FROM
PEKIN TO SIKKIM

FROM

PEKIN TO SIKKIM

THROUGH THE ORDOS, THE
GOBI DESERT, AND TIBET

BY COUNT DE LESDAIN

WITH MAPS AND ILLUSTRATIONS

GYAN

Published by

GYAN

Gyan Publishing House
5, Ansari Road
Daryaganj, New Delhi-110002
Phone: 011-47034999, 9811692060
E-mail: books@gyanbooks.com

Distribution Network
gyanbooks.com
India, USA, Canada, UK, Australia, France

ISBN : 978-81-212-3415-3 (PB)
First Published, 1908

2nd Impression 2020

Printed at: Gyan Press, Delhi.

Pekin to Sikkim
Author: Count De Lesdain

FROM

PEKIN TO SIKKIM

THROUGH THE ORDOS, THE GOBI DESERT, AND TIBET

BY COUNT DE LESDAIN

WITH MAPS AND ILLUSTRATIONS

NEW YORK
E. P. DUTTON AND COMPANY
1908

THE BRITISH CEMETERY AT GYANTSE.

[*Frontispiece.*

TO

J. CLAUDE WHITE, Esq., C.I.E.,

POLITICAL AGENT IN SIKKIM, BHUTAN, AND TIBET

EN SOUVENIR D'AMITIÉ

PREFACE

As the sheets of this book are finally passing through the press the author has been unexpectedly called away to South America, and has asked me to write a preface for it.

The journey performed by the Comte and Comtesse de Lesdain was a remarkable one, all the more so from its having been their wedding tour. That a lady of nineteen should have faced and sustained the hardships of travel in a wild and unknown region described in these pages, can hardly fail to arouse a feeling of admiration and surprise in the mind of the reader.

The journey took place in 1904 - 1905, and lasted seventeen months. It "was undertaken to gratify our wish to cross country hitherto unknown, and if possible to increase the geographical knowledge of our day."

Starting from Pekin, Count de Lesdain struck west to the Hoang-Ho, in order to explore the little known region of the Ordos Desert, which lies in the almost rectangular bend of that mighty river. The region is governed by a number of kinglets, forming the Confederation of the Ordos.

Amongst other spots visited in this part of the journey was Edchen Koro, which contains the tomb of Jenghis Khan, so jealously guarded by its custodians that no European has hitherto been able to discover its actual site, much less to see it.

After traversing the districts of Shansi and Kansu and the Alashan Mountains, the party skirted the Gobi Desert and the Zaidam district, crossing a part of the Kuen-lun range into Tibet, and then travelled over the Dangla (where they encamped at a height of 19,300 feet), past the Tengri-nor Lake, to the Lhasa high road.

It will be seen that the route taken, generally, lies parallel to that traversed by Captain Younghusband on the North, and that taken by Mr R. F. Johnston on the South, and that it touches on many regions which are unknown or scarcely known to Europeans.

JOHN MURRAY.

January, 1908.

CONTENTS

LIST OF ILLUSTRATIONS

THE GREAT WALL OF CHINA, NEAR PEKIN.

[*To face p.* 1.

FROM PEKIN TO SIKKIM THROUGH GOBI AND TIBET

CHAPTER I

FROM PEKIN TO KWEI-HUA-CHENG

ALL departures from Pekin are alike. I had left the capital of the Celestial Empire two years before to make a journey of exploration for some months across the north of Shansi and Central Mongolia. There was then the same scene of animation and bustle in the streets and at the main gates, with a touch of colour here and there to relieve the eyes. Pekin, one of the dirtiest towns on earth, is usually only worth seeing just after dawn, when the rising sun imparts a look of freshness to all things, or in the evening, when on the occasion of some feast thousands of paper lanterns are lighted on all sides.

On the morning of 20th June 1904 the heat was overpowering. Not a breath of wind stirred the still and heavy air. The road, well known to tourists, which runs to the Tombs of the Mings and the Great Wall, and which also leads to Kalgan, was, at eight o'clock in the morning, already hidden under a dense cloud of dust.

We took with us only three Chinese springless carts at the beginning of this expedition, which were amply sufficient for our baggage. As a long journey lay before us we had had to give up the comforts which can be taken in an expedition lasting for a few weeks, or only two or three months. We had decided to live on the resources of the countries through which we proposed to pass, and a few bottles of champagne, for the due celebration of supreme events, were almost the whole stock of our provisions. In Chinese travel, moreover, one can always obtain beef, mutton, chickens, an occasional duck, eggs, flour, and a sufficient supply of vegetables. The explorer is consequently not to be pitied overmuch. The main point is to have with one a good cook. The cook, whom we had with much difficulty recruited in Pekin, was an Annamite. Very clever at his own business, he proved eventually to be a hopeless drunkard. The other servants were a *mafou*, to look after the horses, and some coolies.

I shall not weary the reader with a detailed account of the five days' journey between Pekin and Süen-hua-fu. Many authors have described it. For years diplomatists and tea merchants travelling from Europe to Pekin have gone by Urga, Kalgan, and Süen - hua - fu. However, I should advise those who use this road hereafter to stop at the little town of Hang-ling-tse. A temple on the top of a comparatively high mountain commands the whole vast plain, and from its stony platform one enjoys a magnificent view. In spite of our long day's march we resolved to climb up to it, and with this object sent our men to commandeer donkeys. The temple itself is extremely small, and contains only unimportant statues, but to reach it a wonderful little stony bridge has to be crossed, ornamented with inscriptions and spanning a cleft in the rock. The custodian offered us tea, and refused the small tip which I proffered for his kindness, an experience new to me after Pekin. On our way down we stopped for a few minutes at another temple, larger and newer, where forty lamas at prayer made a great noise in the dimness of the chill and lofty hall of worship.

I must not omit to record that the evening before we chanced upon an exhibition worthy of Barnum's circus. In broad noonday our carters, overcome by the heat, had begged for a short rest, and while they lay stretched under the shade of a tree I had made my way towards a group of Chinese peasants at no great distance off. As I approached I saw one of the tallest men conceivable. He was then seated surrounded by a group of laughing and jesting children, but when he saw me he rose, and I could see that he outtopped all present by some two feet in height. I went and fetched my bag of anthropological instruments, and when I returned began to take the measurements of this colossus. But his mother, a wrinkled old lady, intervened. She said she feared that I should cast an evil spell over her son. The sight of a small ingot of silver, however, successfully calmed her and banished her fears, and I was allowed to proceed with my measurement of her son. His height was fully 8 feet, and a hump detracted from his full measurement in this direction. The circumference of his chest, including the hump, was 58 inches, and the length of his foot 15 inches. Although only twenty-eight years old he had thick white hair, and his whole outward appearance was that of a being whose muscular force and bodily weight were not in proportion.

We reached Süen-hua-fu on the 26th June, and did not stay there long. The town itself has no objects of interest, and the heat had developed in it smells worse than those of Pekin itself, and this fact alone was reason enough to hurry on. We had been well received at the Kon-kuan, or *yamen*, reserved for Mandarins on tour, but as our arrival was wholly unexpected, we had the pleasure of finding in each of our sleeping rooms beggars, wrapped in noisome rags, who were smoking opium, with the tacit approval of the keepers of the house.

On leaving this prefectoral city, instead of making for Kalgan, we branched off slightly to the left and crossed the river Yung-ting-ho or (Hun-ho), nearly dry at this season, with a bed of enormous extent, and made of fine sand yielding here and there beneath our tread. The country that we now reached, west of the river, has the desolate appearance of a bare plain, in which, however, thanks to

A CHINESE GIANT.

[*To face p.* 4.

a constant struggle against bad soil, small villages have struck root and relieve the monotony of the district. Moreover, this wretched appearance does not extend far, and after recrossing the river and reaching Chai-ku-pu one is struck with wonder at the magnificent cultivation which meets the eye. An island in the centre of the river is specially fertile. On all sides there are to be seen fields of poppies of varied colour, richly tinted, pure mauve and deep red, white and cream-coloured. The island looks like fairyland. The irrigation of these fields circled by trees has been devised with much practical skill, and I greatly admire its results. These unlearned Chinese cultivators have taken advantage of almost imperceptible differences of level to flood their fields with a productive supply of water. Opium costs money, and the town of Chai-ku-pu prospers accordingly. The population, perfectly orderly, consists of about five thousand souls.

Our object being to reach Mongolia at Or-tan-ho by the shortest road, I ordered the caravan to leave the beaten track, and to enter upon a mountainous district bounded on the north-east by the Yung-yang-ho. To do this we crossed the Great Wall, not that in the neighbourhood of Pekin, always visited by tourists, but that which is almost endless in extent, since it is met with in Manchuria and on the border of Kansu, and which traces the limits of the northern frontier of the great empire. This is now hardly a causeway.

It has lost all its splendour and importance. It now retains only the value of a relic of history, but it served through centuries as a sturdy defence. At every pass through which a Mongol invasion might break a way for itself the Great Wall reinforced by a fort stood against the invaders. Thus at the issue of the river Yung-yang on Chinese territory rose five or six hundred years ago the fortified city of Shin-ping-fu, of which we could only recognise the lamentable ruins. Opposite this city the old maps mark a fortress with the name of Ping-yuen-fu. This has entirely disappeared. We could hardly identify the remains of its walls. The general appearance of the country, after leaving the fertile valley of the Yung-yang, is again gloomy and poverty-stricken, and the caravan climbed the mountainous district referred to above, over ground made up of loose stones and dried clay. Through low hills crowned by little deserted temples we reached the top of the funnel facing north-east, at the bottom of which lies Or-tan-ho, reached by a gentle slope. The road has no point worth mentioning, but cultivation prospers again, and is able to support an adequate population.

We reached Or-tan-ho about midday, in great heat, and much to our surprise, in spite of its Mongol name, no single Mongol could be found in the whole of the little town. On the other hand, I observed a large number of persons, more or less in rags, bearing on their back or chest the distinctive insignia of the Boxers. This little centre was, four or five years before, a retreat for brigands during the troubles, and a nursery of the insurrection. From here started the bands which attacked Shi-ying-tse, Or-shi-san-ho, Tai-hai, and several other mission centres. However, thanks to the bravery of certain missionaries possessed of common sense, the brigands were driven back with loss. They had certainly heard of the approaching arrival of our little caravan, and the Boxers of the town had consequently arranged for us a somewhat discouraging reception. In the narrow road which led to the river curses were showered upon us from both sides, the most common being Yang-qui-tye, which means "foreign devils." This is not specially emphatic when standing alone, but the victims of it find this compliment, when too often repeated, very trying to the nerves. We hoped to find peace by closing our doors at the inn, and we were in fact undisturbed at our meal. But as soon as we proceeded to pay our bill a discussion arose, for our host did not hesitate to ask an exorbitant price for the use of his inn and kitchen. I naturally declined to pay anything out of the common, and, perceiving that he could not attain his end unaided, the man threw open the door and showed us, with a view to intimidation, that the courtyard was full of Boxers, whose attitude was unquestionably hostile. Realising the need of haste, I wanted to break a way through the crowd and get our caravan away from the inn.

Unluckily the great gate had been securely closed and we were immediately surrounded by all the people present, who, with the Chinaman's customary treachery, began to press us against a wall till we could no longer stir in any direction. As the situation was becoming serious I drew my revolver and threatened to fire upon the men nearest to me. This produced an absurd commotion and a rapid flight of the whole company. Some, since the exit was closed, climbed over the walls, others took refuge in the rooms. My men opened the gates, and the carts crossed the stone threshold. The incident had ended happily. I must say that this was the only occasion on which we met with definite hostility from the inhabitants of a Chinese town.

From Or-tan-ho we made for Or-shi-san-ho, a prosperous mission station in an oasis of verdure surrounded with skilfully cultivated fields and growing woods, a large portion of which have been planted by the missionaries. All this district, like Or-tan-ho and like Shi-ying-tse, has been won by the toiling Chinaman from the indolent Mongol. It is partly the triumph of progress over savagery, and if the Chinaman, rich and poor, were not in the thrall of many vices, and specially of opium, there would be no limit to his activity which would extend the success that a frugal and patient people can always command.

Leaving Or-shi-san-ho on 1st July, we made our way southwards to Ta-tung-fu, one of the largest towns of Shansi. None of the intervening country had yet been visited by a European explorer, but, thanks to the old maps of the Jesuits, a German publisher had been able to publish a practically accurate sketch of it. From the beginning of the day the road ran through mountains and valleys, across low hills and shallow declivities; very numerous but nearly dried up streams all ran towards the Yung-yang-ho. The people seemed poor, and the land very barren. Towards evening we rose about 2,000 feet, and in a narrow little valley discovered the insignificant temple of Lan-ye-miao. As it offered no accommodation for the night we decided to pitch our tent near a group of cottages on the right, a little below the temple.

The road continuing southwards next day merged in the bed of the river Yutto, which is a tributary of the Sang-kan-ho, itself a tributary of the Yung-ting-ho. The volume of the Yutto is considerable, and must, in the rainy season, reach a high level, judging from the marks it leaves on the rocks, between which it forces its way. Early on the 3rd July we reached some very interesting ruins of the Great Wall. Clearly, the Chinese strategists apprehended here more than elsewhere an invasion from the Yutto Valley, for they multiplied defences at this point. Over a stretch of 4 miles I counted the remains of eighty bastions, some built up against the wall, while others stood out in front like pickets, and could take the enemy in the rear, if, after passing the first line of defence, they should reach the wall. The wall itself must have reached a great height, and, as I noticed here alone, it is perpendicular on the Mongol side, and gently sloping on the Chinese. By the irony of fate the inhabitants of the district have dug out of the mounds of earth that form the slope stables for their cattle. Three miles away from the wall rise the ruins of an old fortified city, which are remarkable only for an ancient triumphal arch, and a gate in the ramparts, made of hewn stone, and strikingly well built. Still following the bed of the same river we reached Ta-tung-fu on the following day. This important place deserves special mention.

Ta-tung-fu was very strongly fortified, and its defences are still imposing. Its shape is rectangular, and it has four gates strengthened by double walls. The northern gate, in old days the point of danger, does not communicate directly with the plain, but opens into a strong citadel, a miniature copy of the city itself. In this are the parade ground and the barracks of the troops, recognisable from the number of small flags that surmount them. I think I may assert that the Chinese forces retain ancient forms not yet Westernised; for example, there is one flag to every ten men.

The interior of the city contains some triumphal arches, in the purest Chinese style, and great main streets comprising shops well furnished for the interior of a Chinese province. Particularly well preserved also is a great wall covered with coloured tiles representing a dragon. The tint of these tiles is very fine, and no European factory can produce richer work.

We did not stay long at Ta-tung-fu, for we wished to reach the desert of the Ordos as soon as possible, and purely Chinese towns did not interest us overmuch. If it is true to assert that all the cities of the Celestial Empire are alike, it is a different story with the temples, for we visited on the day after our departure from Ta-tung-fu the most interesting and curious temples that we ever had the fortune to see—I mean the grottoes of Yung-yang-miao.

To reach them one must travel along the picturesque valley of the Shi-li-ho for some dozen miles, and pass before a small but very striking temple whose entrance gate is guarded from the wrong-doing of the ill-affected by a wall covered with tiles in a style similar to those I described at Ta-tung-fu. Its roof is also coated with coloured tiles. Soon after, the village of Che-kon-han-chu is reached, where two chapels, which call for notice, are cut out of the rock. They consist of two square chambers, the vault above being supported by a central rectangular pillar. I concluded that they existed first as natural grottoes caused by the passage of water, and that the Chinese had only enlarged them and shaped them as they are to-day. In one of them a spring which rises with a weak flow supports this theory. They show otherwise clear traces of water action. To a height of some 3 feet the friable rock has crumbled, and the ceilings of both chambers are entirely mildewed. Though now in poor preservation, they remain a proof of some considerable sculptural achievement. Each room contains over a thousand figures, some nearly 6 feet high, others only a few inches. The ceilings especially are a maze of painted dragons. The statues also were painted, but are now discoloured by the effects of the water. However, Buddhist piety has succeeded in repairing some of the figures, especially the statue of a Turk, in a turban crowned with an aureole, in the first room, whose presence seems a tasteless anachronism. I concluded that gates, which have perished, originally closed the entry. As to the inscription in the interior of these grottoes goodwill alone could not suffice to decipher them.

A little further on are the village and temple of Yung-yang, made up of grottoes all cut out by human hand in a great wall of limestone reaching for three-quarters of a mile on the bank of the Chi-li-ho. They are many hundreds in number, and all contain a seated Buddha carved in the living rock. The nearest to Ta-tung-fu are the only important ones. They are very lofty and adorned on the outside with wooden temples three and four stories in height. These

THE TEMPLE OF YUNG-YANG-MIAO.

[*To face p.* 12.

stories are connected by staircases cut in the rock, and are composed of platforms of which the highest are on a level with the eyes of the Buddha. These Buddhas are huge, and are surrounded by small figures like the angels round the central figure over the altar of a Roman Catholic Church. The general appearance of the temple is not unlike a theatre, of which the grotto serves as the stage. In one of these grottoes a Buddha 50 feet high is entirely gilded, and wears on his forehead a crown of coloured glass. His eyes also are made of glass. The wooden temples were repainted twenty years ago, and are consequently very conspicuous and picturesque. Unluckily money was apparently lacking to renew the platforms and railings, and I should not advise any one to approach too near to the abyss to get a close view of the statue, which is very striking as seen either from above or below.

The other grottoes have no temples in front, and the largest, which contain some gilded statues adorned with imitation gems, are simply divided from the outside by wooden bars. The smaller grottoes have not even these. Legend, in the mouth of the old lama in charge, insists that all once had their temples in front, but some thousand years ago, he avers, a deluge of twelve days' rain loosened the foundations of the temples, even then ancient, and reduced them practically to ruins. Seven days after the rain, an unknown man stood before the temples, and with uplifted arm gave them the order to fall. All fell together, exposing the grottoes as they may be seen to-day. The truth is, that, if these porticos ever existed, they fell one after another for the all-sufficient reason that the Chinese, who occasionally repaint, never restore or rebuild.

After a four days' march we reached So-ping-fu on 9th July, having followed from the temples of Yung-yang, a high road wholly without interest, and only remarkable for the large number of old towns and fortified villages, completely deserted and abandoned, telling the sad story of the real China of to-day, infinitely less populous and industrious, whatever may be said, than it was three hundred years ago. So-ping-fu hardly deserves to be called a prefecture. It is a dead city. Its empty streets form a melancholy contrast to the activity of Ta-tung-fu. We stayed there one night only, and spent it in the house of a tea merchant, the inns being too repulsive.

The next day we set out with an escort of six grotesque soldiers, armed with absurd knives and with sticks. Having drawn one of these terrible swords from its sheath I found the blade to be made of wood, and the warrior quite shamelessly explained to me that he had sold the steel that he might buy opium.

Our purpose was to go from So-ping-fu to the Ordos by way of Cha-ber-noor, where lived a missionary friend of ours, a man of enlightenment. We had travelled together two years before, and I was looking forward to seeing him again. There is no direct road from So-ping-fu to Cha-ber-noor. We had either to take the high road to Kwei-hua-cheng, or, having reached the little town of Shakolo, to try to make a way along the river Ulan-muren, which has a bad repute, amply justified by its quicksands. We decided for the latter course, which was more difficult, but more novel, and started for Shakolo, a very pretty little town at the opening of a defile. In older days the river Ulan-muren, which washes its walls and is a tributary of the Yellow River, was defended by a fortified bridge with very narrow stone arches, which, spanning the stream here and there, prevented the passage of troops in the shallow water. Only the ruins of this interesting work now remain on the left bank of the river.

We arrived at Cha-ber-noor after a march along the Ulan-muren, which was not without incidents. It was not easy to get our baggage carts along the banks which were strewn with large boulders, and when we had overcome this trouble we found ourselves encountered by treacherous quicksands. I nearly disappeared myself in one of these deceptive spots while searching for a place at which we could cross the river. Taken in by the colour of the ground, I forced my horse forward against his wish, and found myself about 3 feet deep in mud. Luckily, I was riding an exceptionally vigorous pony. Roused and inspired by the instinct of self-preservation more than by my riding-whip, he managed, after a series of struggles, to get clear of the quicksand.

The first 20 or 30 miles of the course of the Ulan-muren are very thinly populated, and almost given up to the pasturage of sheep and goats. An incalculable number of hares are also to be found here. As they are not wild they are easily killed. Near a hamlet called San-chou-long I remember knocking over a dozen of these animals in the little clearings between the scanty bushes in less than ten minutes. It proved to be a waste of powder and shot, for our men refused to eat their flesh. A deep-rooted superstition convinces them that the souls of their grandparents reside after death in the bodies of hares.

After leaving the Ulan-muren we crossed a small hilly district 1,200 feet in height, and debouched upon the huge plain of Tumet, in which are Cha-ber-noor, a number of flourishing villages, and the great city of Kwei-hua-cheng.

Hardly had the Mandarins of this last place, with whom I had often been brought into contact two years before, heard of our presence at Cha-ber-noor, than they sent us pressing invitations to come to Kwei-hua-cheng. Although this digression did not quite suit our plans, I decided to comply with their request, hoping to obtain from them letters of recommendation, and greater facilities for crossing the Ordos. One of these Mandarins, who rejoices in the title of the Tartar

Marshal, is the real head of the Ordos, of Tumet, and of Northern Mongolia. He represents the Pekin Government among the Mongol princes, and exercises great influence from this fact.

But before starting for the Blue Town I had been obliged to make some changes on the staff of our caravan. Having obtained clear evidence of the thefts of which the *mafou* had been guilty, I had dismissed this gentleman, not without having recovered, quite by chance, some of the stolen property, among which was a bottle of mercury which I had brought for astronomical observations.

Furthermore, all the information which I had received latterly about travel in the Ordos, and about the condition of the roads there, had made it clear to me that I should only be able to use my Pekin carts for a very short time, and accordingly I had decided to send them back at once and to buy some camels. At Kwei-hua-cheng in the summer good camels can be bought in the market for a sum varying from 40 to 50 *taels*. For the kind of work which the animals had to do it was important that they should be very fat, and not too young. In fact, instead of travelling by night to avoid the heat, as the Chinese and Mongols always do, we had decided that we would cover our stages by day-light, preferring to sacrifice the animals rather than our sleep. Mongolian camels do not bear heat well, and the hot sun is sometimes actually overwhelming when reflected from the sand and beating on the Ordos in August. The chief cause is that the long hair of the camels induce an abnormal perspiration, which rapidly makes them thin, and then their loads produce huge abscesses, which render them useless. On the other hand, they are not accustomed to eat at night, but only during the day, and when they halt after a hot stage they are so wearied by the heat that they stretch themselves on the sand and rest rather than eat the grass close by.

In such circumstances their health fails quickly, but in spite of these drawbacks, provided that their feet do not sink in the sand or the mud, they are the best animals for crossing the Ordos with.

We started then for Kwei-hua-cheng with a small troop of camels and a new staff. The road from Cha-ber-noor is flat, and very easy, and we met with no difficulty. We were accordingly perfectly fit and not at all tired when we established ourselves in the Kon-kuan, which had been reserved for us. We started almost at once upon a series of sumptuous dinners, at which the dishes were as numerous as they were indigestible, while the feast was heralded, interrupted, and followed, by performances of Chinese minstrels and jugglers, which were very entertaining.

I remember especially a little man, full of activity and good humour, who swallowed a fiery ball somewhat larger than his fist, and made grotesque gestures while his deeply impressed audience watched the ball gradually descend to the level of his stomach. After a few minutes he made the solid mass rise to his mouth again apparently with consummate ease. Another man swung on a trapeze made of swords between two trees, and managed not to cut his hands on the sharp blades.

But by far the most interesting exhibition which we witnessed was a review of troops, newly drilled by a Chinese officer, who had received lessons from the Germans at Tientsin in military movements and tactics. I must own that he had profited by his lessons, and had reached an altogether remarkable result with the soldiers entrusted to him by the Mandarins of Kwei-hua-cheng. Five hundred of them performed all the exercises in which the men of European regiments are daily drilled. They wore a smart uniform of dark hue, absolutely different from the long robes and the *impedimenta* of all kinds that Chinese soldiers usually affect. Oddly enough the General, and the many officers of this regiment, had retained the pale yellow or sky-blue gauze robes, and seemed quite out of place amidst their men, who were rapidly manœuvring at the command of their instructor.

I do not venture to assert that the soldiers of Kwei-hua-cheng are at this moment to be dreaded, especially if they were to be confronted by European troops. No doubt, on the battle-field they would quickly forget the fine precision of their drill and the spirit of discipline so hardly inculcated, but, notwithstanding, the fact of finding in the north of Shansi an instructor and well drilled men seems to me worthy of notice.

Indubitably the Chinese are making efforts to raise the level of their troops. In the neighbourhood of Pekin, Yuen-chi-kai, with Japanese help, has set up a real army, and no doubt these men enlisted from Japanese, and even from Europeans, armed with Mannlicher rifles of German make, will prove in future their superiority to their absurd, barbarous, cowardly, and undisciplined predecessors. Add to this the consideration that the Japanese triumph over Russia has puffed them up with pride. Everywhere, even in the most remote town of Kansu, the Chinese people know all about the decisive defeat of the Russian arms, and as they draw no distinction between a Muscovite, a Frenchman, or an Englishman, but class them all under one heading, the defeat of one entails a loss of prestige on all. I found many proofs of this in all directions. But this is not the place to discuss the future. I am content to assert, and I shall not be contradicted by those who have studied the new state of affairs, that the next war with China will cost more lives than any of its predecessors, and will raise more difficulties than the European nations, more or less allied, have yet had to overcome.

After the review we were invited to partake of a light repast in the General's summer residence.

It is in the Manchu city. Kwei-hua-cheng, in fact, comprises two very distinct towns close together. The first, in which we were lodged, and in which I had previously spent nearly two months, is Chinese, laid out without apparent plan, and very dirty. The second is well ventilated by avenues of great trees, under which the homes of the poorest seem less wretched than elsewhere; contains some large *yamens*, and is inhabited by the Manchu aristocracy.

The house in which we were entertained was composed only of a few very small rooms, and lunch was laid under a blue tent pitched between the dwelling-house and the garden. This last, without being extensive, contained a great variety of flowers, which we had to inspect, for our host was very proud of them. Owing to the special gift possessed by the Chinese of planning a garden in a picturesque style, and ornamenting the most ordinary spots with taste and novelty, the general effect was very artistic.

This was the last of the official entertainments offered us by the Mandarins, and, our preparations being completed, we decided to set out without delay to cross the Ordos. On the morning of our departure the Prefect came to visit us, and enquired of me very confidentially whether there would be a little rain. "I know," he said, "that Europeans have constructed instruments by which they can foretell drought or rain. For a long time not a drop of rain has fallen in the surrounding country, and I have to go to the temple and offer up public prayers to the gods. But if the drought persists when I have done this, I shall look somewhat foolish! Can you give me the slightest hint?" I laughed, and replied that the barometer had gone down considerably, and that he might pray to the gods with every confidence that his prayer would be heard.

Escorted by the good Prefect we started off, and a little later he left us to go to the temple.

I was a true prophet, for in the course of the day we received several showers—more beneficial to the crops than pleasant for travellers.

CHAPTER II

THE ORDOS

BEFORE beginning the account of our crossing of the Ordos Desert, I think it well to give the reader a short description of it. This part of the world has been seldom visited, and as it is marked as a desert on all the maps, many people no doubt think it absolutely barren, without life and out of all touch with relation to the rest of China or Mongolia. The Ordos have a curious resemblance in shape to the Spanish Peninsula. The nearest point to Pekin is at a distance of fifteen days' journey; but couriers can reach the capital of the Celestial Empire in less than a hundred hours, thanks to the relays of good ponies, which are much quicker and more active than the short and squat animals generally ridden by the Tibetans and Bhutans.

The Yellow River, Hoang-Ho, is the natural boundary which encircles the Ordos on the west, north, and east, and, at certain seasons of the year, makes them almost inaccessible to travellers from the north. On the south, the provinces of Shansi and Kansu, bounded by the Great Wall, or at least what remains of it, mark the limit which the inhabitants must not cross for fear of losing their apparent independence.

Shut in, therefore, on all sides, the population of Mongol tribes, scattered over this country, incorrectly termed desert, has not been able to extend, but has collected at certain fixed points when the nature of the ground and the larger quantity of rain allow of the rearing of sheep, oxen, and horses, often in very large numbers. This is the reason why the density of the population is much greater there than elsewhere in Mongolia, why the trade with China is more active, and why the Chinese Mandarins draw a large revenue from the Ordos. Even if the Mongols were to cross their natural frontier, the Yellow River, and to try to spread in all directions in search of rich pasture grounds, they would be stopped on the north-east by the Chinese, who have conquered little by little, by force of patience, from other Mongol tribes, the rich plains of Tumet, and the alluvial land left on the north by the old beds of the river. On the west, they would run against a real sandy desert, barren and deadly, and if they succeeded in crossing it, they would have to fight with the sovereign prince of Kokonor and king of Alashan, at present residing at Fu-ma-fu.

The climate of the Ordos is good and preferable to that of the huge steppes of Mongolia. The average height, about 4,500 feet, provides a plateau on which the intensity of the summer

THE CARAVAN CROSSING THE ULAN MUREN DESERT OF ORDOS.

[*To face p.* 24.

heat is not felt so severely as in Alashan in the same latitude. This plateau, without great mountains or deep valleys, is furrowed by a few water-courses, tributaries of the Yellow River, and almost all flowing eastward. Their beds are sometimes very wide, the bottom of them is of fine sand, often shifting and perilous; but it is rare to find more than a foot of water in the largest river in summer. The inhabitants have come to think nothing of the little streams which cross their country, and the water which they drink always comes from wells or from muddy swamps left by the rains. This is obviously an unwholesome drink, and the peculiar smell of some swamps would make the whole faculty of medicine shudder. But here, as everywhere, habit is stronger than science, and the Mongols, who often drink the water just as they find it, when they have no time to boil their tea, feel no evil effects from it. On the contrary, the people seem remarkably energetic, and their individual constitutions are as strong as possible. Unluckily, the custom of opium-smoking is slowly gaining ground, especially near Tumet, and is rapidly extending its ravages. Their energy is failing, life is dying out, and I have seen some Mongol Mandarins whose haggard faces and deeply-lined features reminded one of the worst Chinese smokers.

The Mongols are, as is well known, divided into two great political parties. One ranges itself under the ancient banners, the other obeys chiefs who bear the pompous titles of kings, and all claim to be descended from the companions, or even the family, of Jenghis Khan. The Mongols of the banners inhabit the huge steppes which stretch even further than Kalgan to the east, up to Urga in the north, and as far as Tumet on the west.

The country of the Ordos is governed by a confederation of kinglets, five in number, who live on good enough terms with each other. The oldest, not he who has reigned the longest, is Chief of the confederation, and treats directly with the representative of the Pekin Government who lives at Kwei - hua - cheng, or in the Mongol tongue, Ku - ku - Hoto. The title of this high officer, generally a Manchu, is that of Tartar Marshal. He has power enough to enable him to exercise a good deal of injustice, thanks to which he fills his coffers in preference to those of the State. Under the Kings, but with more real power, some important lamas (ta lama) govern the people by working upon their grossly superstitious minds, and are here, as in Tibet, the true masters of the situation.

After this long prelude, which I hope may be forgiven, I resume the account of our expedition.

Being thoroughly furnished with letters of recommendation and imperative passports for the Mongol Princes, we set out towards the end of July, for the ruined town of Tu-tchrung, not far from which we were to cross the Yellow River in boats specially prepared for the purpose. More important than all these paper precautions, the Tartar Marshal had sent with us one of his secretaries, with orders to commandeer for us all the requisite means of transport; and I found this fashion of travelling very pleasant.

After two days' march from Kwei-hua we arrived at the banks of the Yellow River, just in time to witness the complete destruction of several villages ingulfed in the huge annual flood. During two journeys, I have had opportunities of studying the disastrous floods of this great artery of Asia, so I may be allowed another digression on this subject.

The Yellow River rises in Tibet, not far from Lake Oring, in a high water-shed, on which the snow collects in winter in large quantities. Before entering Mongolia it passes a series of water-sheds which, joined to those of Tibet, produce an enormous volume of water when the snows melt. As long as this liquid mass flows in a channel shut in by rocks it obviously cannot spread and do damage, but when it reaches the huge plains of the North of Alashan, of the Ordos, and especially Tumet, where the fall is less marked, it loses in depth but gains enormously in breadth. What also contributes largely towards this change is a defile situated about 40° S. lat., and not far from Ho-Kau. At the point the rocks contract the river-banks to such an extent as not to leave a wide enough passage in the summer. I should think it would be comparatively easy to widen this opening by means of dynamite, and in this way to diminish the disasters caused all along the previous course of the river. Whether this may be the case or not, as regards the future, the ravages of the annual floods at present are frightful. It is useless for the peasants to dig ditches several feet wide round their mud-built houses, nothing can withstand the invading element, nothing arrest its advance. Little by little the water makes its way, undermining and bursting the dykes.

The cottages collapse in an instant, and with them the harvest laid out to dry on the roofs. This is the history of thousands of peasants who, evicted by the flood, come back and build the same house, and cultivate the same field to see them once more become the prey of the flood. The obstinacy of the Chinese is unrivalled. All the country round the spot at which we reached the river-bank was a swamp. Here and there a few trees and a few roofs, which had not yet fallen, were visible, and the sheet of water was more than 3 or 4 miles broad.

Except for these floods, which sometimes make navigation difficult, and, above all, render it impossible to fix on any definite landing-places, it would be a profitable enterprise with the help of the Mandarins, always a doubtful quantity, to establish a service of steam tugs which would

A WELL IN THE ALASHAN DESERT.

[*To face p.* 28.

make much money by hauling the numberless boats, which carry the products of Kansu to Kwei-hua-cheng.

Being unable to cross the river at this point, we made for Ho-Kau, where we arrived after a day's journey, after passing the imposing ruins of Tu-tchrung, which was a noble stronghold in the days of the Nestorian civilisation, and the splendour of which Marco Polo has celebrated. To-day a few grass mounds inside its circuit barely mark the heap of ruins of some important dwelling, and the cattle of the peasants eat the shrubs that are growing over the turrets.

Ho-Kau is not a safe place in flood-time. The contracted bed of the river causes the current to impinge with terrible pressure against the dykes protecting the town, which is built below the water-level, and a single breach in the protection works would be enough to destroy it. The level of the flood, having been particularly high this year, almost the whole of the population had fled, and it was with a sense of deliverance that we left this town on the morning of the 28th July.

Our only difficulty in crossing the river was the objection of the camels to venture upon the moving tide. We had to employ a great number of coolies, and lift the legs of the camels one by one into the barge, to overcome their obstinacy. On the other bank we were at once amongst sand hills, and at nightfall we stopped at a hamlet composed of the wretched huts.

Our intention was to cross the Ordos in a diagonal line, coming out at Ning-hsia in the Province of Kansu. On the way we meant to visit four of the Mongol Kings, and to see the venerated monument which covers the remains of the greatest conqueror that the world has known —Jenghis Khan.

The road to the Palace of Chongar, the first of these princes, runs through a succession of sand-hills; of plains partly cultivated by Chinese peasants, and of rocky ground. One river only, the Eul Ru Ho, flowing to the north-east, crosses the plateau, and in the month of July the water in it is not more than 5 or 6 inches deep.

A few years ago the palace stood in a different place. Probably the pasturage grew worse, and the then reigning prince transferred the seat of his government to another plain. On reaching the top of a little eminence we suddenly came in sight of several buildings, which, standing in an almost complete desert, appeared magnificent. These were the palaces. The King's palace is surrounded by ruined walls 18 feet high, with two entrances, of which the southern leads straight to the royal buildings. These consist simply of a large Chinese house, built in the favourite style, with three central courts, with carved wooden windows, and small panes of glass replaced here and there by pieces of paper. The walls and the courts are of brick, which gives the whole dwelling a comfortable appearance. Not far away some flags and prayers, written on small pieces of cloth, marked the temple where, on great occasions, the Prince offers sacrifices, such as an outbreak of cattle disease, of drought, or when his business is not prospering at the Court of Pekin.

The Prince soon came to visit us. We had hardly settled in a wing of his palace when he appeared, dressed in official costume, and followed by a train of dirty Ministers. A sheep boiled whole was put before us, which is a mark of honour in Mongolia, and the dinner was cooked in a style which he fancied to be European. In answer to my questions about the Tomb of Jenghis Khan, he assured me that I was a long way from it, that it was inaccessible, and that no one had the key to it. His predecessor, who was visited by the French explorer, Charles Bonin, in 1898, during a few days' visit to the Ordos, was much inclined to do kindnesses to Europeans. He was the first to announce to my fellow-countrymen the exact date of the Boxer movement, and of the attack on the Legations at Pekin. Bonin made it his duty to inform his Legation immediately, which, of course, instead of taking measures, or at least making enquiries and warning the other Legations, treated Bonin as a lunatic, put his letters in a pigeon-hole, forgot them, and was attacked at the appointed time.

I mention this fact, which does not stand alone, simply to prove that what happened in China in 1900 might have been avoided, and that much bloodshed might have been spared.

The former Prince of Chongar did not inhabit this new dwelling, but had built for himself a very pretty little palace a little further north and outside the ramparts, carefully constructed and surrounded by a kind of park. In one of the inner courts were ornamental pools and fountains —true luxury in the Ordos. One or two of the many wives he left behind him are now living there, and spending the rest of their days in regrets for the time past, and in smoking opium.

The reigning Prince is married to quite a young woman. He has only one lawful wife, but he has generously offered hospitality to his aunt and her daughter. We went to see them, and I do not think that I ever met with a stronger smell of opium in a Chinese house than in the room of these two women. They live an entirely useless and unoccupied life, and one wonders how they escape utter boredom.

As the sun was setting, the Prime Minister insisted that we should visit the *yamen* of justice, and we complied with his wish. This *yamen*, of which he seemed very proud, was a wretched place, its only furniture being a strong box made of carved wood, heavily strengthened with iron bars, and chains intended for criminals. The strong box is empty, and the chains rusted,

THE PALACE OF THE PRINCE OF TCHONGAR.

[*To face p.* 32.

for there is little crime in the Ordos, and when it does happen the murderer always escapes. In the evening we received another dinner sent by the Prince, and the following morning we left the palace, escorted by Mandarins, and by soldiers armed with blunt knives and home-made guns, long, slender, and equipped with rickety wooden stocks. They are fired from a fork like the Tibetan guns, and are only effective at a very short range.

The Palace of Chongar, simple as it was, afterwards seemed to us a marvel, compared with the poverty and smallness of those which we visited subsequently.

Our guide had been ordered to take us to the King Wangtse. Every attempt to draw the conversation to the subject of the Tomb of Jenghis Khan was coldly received, and as all the answers were evidently untruthful, I thought it politic on my part to seem to give up the idea. I relied upon the directions left by Bonin, upon chance—and upon strategy—to attain my end.

Our road ran west, and crossed a large number of moderate-sized and small rivers. The country was by no means such as could be called a desert. There were fields, cottages, crops drying in the sun, in all the many little valleys which we had to cross. This portion of the Ordos is populated and fertile, and plenteously rewards the labour of its cultivators. These latter are all Chinese, who have generally met with a series of misfortunes in their own country, have fallen out with their Mandarins, and have come to seek shelter, food, and peace under the banner of a Mongol Prince, who on his part gains a double advantage from their settlement in his little kingdom.

These settlers afford a means of imposing taxes, however small, and of buying on the spot the corn which the people use, at a much cheaper rate than he would get in the Chinese market. The Mongol is in fact the prey of the Chinese, since his simplicity and his astounding idleness make him a pigeon easy to pluck. He never keeps a shop, or cultivates the ground; these occupations are too servile for him. He never works a mine, for that would bring on him the curses of the mountain genie, and in short owing to his pride, laziness, and superstition, he never obtains any advantage from the natural richness of the ground. The only occupation which he considers worthy of his lofty origin is the bearing of arms. Pekin pays each Mongol soldier a very small salary, which is enough for his immediate wants, and to meet any further requirements he sells his horses or his sheep to the Chinese merchants, who are constantly crossing the country in all directions. In the Ordos the normal price of a good horse, not an ambler, is from 10 to 15 *taels*. Animals which have been taught to amble, and do it well, reach a much higher figure, from 40 to 50 *taels*. A sheep costs 1 *tael*, and an ox 5 or 6.

After some stages, and a two days' halt near a little Chinese village, in consequence of a sudden attack of fever, I had reason to suppose that I was very close to the Tomb of the great Emperor, and without arousing the suspicions of my Mongol escort, I approached a group of Chinamen, and asked where Edchen Koro was, for this is the Mongol name of that sacred place. They replied, "You are not a day's march from it. If you take this road you will get there to-night." I ordered a start to be made at once, and instead of pursuing the road which my guides were pressing me to take, I took the road for Edchen Koro. Their pitiable faces amused us very much for some minutes, and one of them disappeared to carry to the Prince of Chongar the disastrous news of our visit to the tombs.

The sun in fact was still high in the heavens, when we distinguished at a turn of the road which had been running through hilly country since morning, a plain and unadorned white mass, with two gilded balls above it. This was Edchen Koro. The Tomb is situated on the eastern side of a small hill, some 50 yards above a wretched village, where lives the custodian who has charge of the keys. It faces south, and is raised on a terrace some 3 feet high. A palisade of posts fixed at intervals surrounds the terrace, and in it is a single crumbling and worm-eaten gate opening towards the south. The general aspect of the tomb is so poverty-stricken that one feels a painful shock in traversing this miserable entrance of what may be called the Tabernaculum. Two small tents, one behind the other, and connected by a very low inner door, made of worn-out felt, and admitting, through their rents, the rain and the wind are the "monument" destined to perpetuate the renown of the greatest conqueror the world has known; and one who in his lifetime possessed a greater extent of territory than any contemporary monarch; whose name spread terror, and commanded obedience from the banks of the Yellow River to the borders of Poland. The ashes of the body of Jenghis Khan are deposited in a kind of chest, cubic in shape, and placed on a wooden support made of small coloured pillars, adorned with paintings on all its sides, except that facing south, which is covered with a finely-worked copper plate representing a divinity surrounded by four animals which are difficult to identify. Each side of this coffin, which serves the purpose of a funeral urn, is adorned with a handle of gilded copper, by which it is raised, and which seemed to me a fit emblem of the eternal migration of one who overran so many countries when alive, and even after his death has not found rest. The Tomb, in fact, has not always been here; but it is difficult to know exactly where the first descendants of the great Emperor laid his remains.

One thing is certain, from the admission of the Mongols themselves, that the tents at Edchen

Koro have been comparatively recently set up. They have not the slightest idea of who Jenghis Khan was, and of their own history they know nothing, of their conquest of the ancient world, of their struggle against China, and of their final defeat for want of organisation; nor do they know the date of Jenghis Khan. The custodian of the tomb, when questioned by me on this matter, replied that at least three thousand years had passed since his death, and when I tried to fix the dates, and to convince him of his mistake, he simply turned his back upon me, and carefully shut the doors of the first tent, which serves as an antechamber, after having put out the tallow lamp which he had lighted when we came in, and which, when he prostrates himself, he raises in his hands.

To conclude, there is very little to see, and still less to admire at Edchen Koro. The tents contain nothing remarkable except the coffin. As everywhere else, in all temples, large and small, coloured flags, dirty and dusty pieces of silk, a few nicknacks, a looking-glass over the coffin, some prayers written on pieces of cloth, and a canopy of silk, easily filled the chief tent, which is only 4½ yards long and 3 yards broad. It is worth noting that this tent was the only felt tent of an oval shape that I saw. As to the first tent, it was absolutely empty.

The territory of Edchen Koro is under the rule of the King of Wangtse, and the key of the coffin itself is deposited in his palace. As to the Mongols trusted to keep the tombs, they form a little tribe called "Targat" (in the Mongol language, "that which pays no taxes"). The fact that they keep watch over the great man's remains exempts them from the slight annual payment that lies heavy on their fellow-countrymen.

I must confess that we expected to find a sumptuous, or at least, a respectable monument, and that the discovery of the real lamentable state of things was a disappointment to us. But for the two gilded balls above them, these two tents would entirely fail to catch the eyes of a traveller.

Soon after leaving Edchen Koro we had a complete change of scenery. Instead of ravines and little hills, divided by very scanty streams, there was a boundless expanse of huge green plains, where flocks abounded, and there were fewer Chinese.

Here and there are some absolutely deserted villages, and we camped the first day in an abandoned spot, where it was difficult to provide for our meals. The Mongol Mandarin, a button of the third rank, of pale blue crystal, whom the Prince of Chongar had ordered to conduct us to his neighbour, and to procure food and shelter for us on the way, was a worthless rascal.

He might have been any age, and, like all opium smokers, had no energy at all. We always had to wait for him in the morning, for he had never finished his opium smoking, and it required all my self-control to restrain me from giving him a thrashing. Through his fault, we found nothing prepared at the end of a stage, and I would rather travel alone than with such a major-domo.

The 20th of August was a specially bad day. Having found my Mandarin absolutely unable to get up in the morning, I took from him his official badges, which gave him the right to commandeer, and left him. On our way, at a place where several roads meet, I forced a Chinaman to guide us, for fear of our mistaking the road. Having received the order without saying a word, the man started off walking in front of our caravan. After 3 or 4 miles, I discovered that he was deaf, and was quietly returning to his own home! As we retraced our steps a violent storm broke upon us, which did not add to the pleasure of the situation. I have observed that in the Ordos, during August, storms occur pretty regularly every three days, and are accompanied by violent lightning; but given certain atmospheric conditions, the clouds are on the level of the earth, and the lightning does not appear in flashes, but rather like a very bright and sudden luminous radiance.

I noticed throughout this country many traces of coal, sometimes on the surface, sometimes exposed by river channels. I doubt whether the veins are very important; but even if they were the finest in the whole world, there are no means of working them remuneratively, in the present difficult conditions of transport in China. I shall have the same to say in another chapter on the mines of Kansu, which have so tempted the King of Belgium that he has sent several engineers to study the mineral riches on the spot, and keeps at Liang-chou a permanent agent, commissioned to obtain acceptable terms from the Governor—by no means an easy thing.

The sudden view of the temple of Chongara T'chao, which rises out of an enormous green plain, and looks like an oasis of tall trees, was a complete surprise to us. Its roofs of coloured tiles, green and yellow, are very striking. The gorge in front of it, formed by a small river, is very picturesque, and the general effect is charming.

This temple, built upon the territory of Wangtse, contains, it appears, more than seven hundred lamas. This would be little for Tibet, but is much for the Ordos, where it is not easy to get together the necessary supplies for a large community. It is a collection of great buildings, part of which have been made after the Tibetan fashion, that is to say, with little square windows painted with dark colours, which contrast with the white walls. The two principal temples stand on brick terraces, and the beams of the entrance are adorned with specially fine painting. Inside the second hall, and on one side of it, is a collection of handsome statues of gilded copper, all dressed in silk draperies, some of them more than 9 feet high. This second temple, or second hall, is built in the Chinese fashion. Three rows of elephants' trunks and tusks support a gabled roof. Before the altars there was the usual offering, cakes of mutton fat, heaps of flour, and bowls of pure water. I tried to buy some of the pictures which adorned the walls, but I could not acquire any at any price. The lamas attach the greatest value to these pictures, often several centuries old, and attribute them to the days of the first disciples of Buddha. While walking across the village, where the houses of the priests stand close together, I noticed many ancient paintings in a remarkable state of preservation. One of them had for its subject Heaven; and the artist had undertaken to represent the pleasures, the walks, the siestas, the dinners, and the prayers which await the good man. Another, on the contrary, represented Hell, and consisted of a wheel pressed between the legs of a frightful-looking genie. In the upper part of this wheel are depicted evil actions, and in the lower part, divided into sixteen little squares, the way in which they are punished.

We were lodged almost comfortably in a great lofty room adorned with tapestries and Ning-hsia carpets, and we hoped to enjoy sound sleep there, but had reckoned without the piety and the religious zeal of the lamas, who were keeping some festival or other, by mumbling and chanting prayers all night. In the morning the chief lama, in his richest vestment of yellow silk, came and presented us with dried dates and butter.

We left Chongara T'chao soon after, and followed a track which crossed a Chao country similar to that which I have already described. It is noticeable here, however, that the Chinese element which is pre-eminent in the territory of Chongar, has almost disappeared on that of Wangtse.

This Wangtse, who is one of the least important in the confederation of the Ordos, showed no consideration whatever for the orders which the Tartar Marshal had sent as to our reception. On hearing of our arrival, he had simply prepared the mud houses, where, by Mongol custom, hospitality is given to pilgrims crossing the country, and going to the holy places, such as Kumbum. Naturally, we could not put up with such cavalier treatment, and, putting spurs to my pony, I rode to the Prince's house. On my arrival I found all the doors shut, but with the assistance of some men I set about opening the chief entrance. The interior of the palace seemed absolutely silent. We had nearly finished our work when one of the Prince's servants came out of a little side door reserved for inferior officers, and asked me to follow him. I replied that I would only enter through the chief gate, and ordered our caravan men to go on with their work. A few minutes later a man came up rather better clothed than the others, and introduced himself as the Prince. He begged me to come in by a small door, for he assured me that the chief gate was never used. But, at this moment, my men had succeeded in opening the closely fastened shutters, strengthened with bars of wood laid horizontally, and I advanced into the chief court of the palace.

It was indeed different from that of Chongar. Instead of the great Chinese court, paved and comparatively clean, it was a square of stamped earth surrounded by walls, and absolutely disgusting. Its only interesting peculiarity was the presence of two Mongol tents, of an ordinary type, under which the Prince lived, rather than in the little Chinese house, containing only three rooms, which he had built on the north of the enclosure, and used only for receptions. We took up our abode quietly in it, and, as all earthly things have their humorous side, we had much pleasure in observing the altercation which took place between the chief of our escort and the Prince. The former, happy to be able to frighten a Mongol with impunity, by picturing the Tartar Marshal's anger, took a very high tone with him, and the wretched Prince pleaded, prayed, and sobbed for more than a quarter of an hour, before our centurion consented to forgive him. I may add that this forgiveness cost the Prince a good round sum.

The territory of Wangtse seemed poverty-stricken. We could not find flour fit to cook, and only after a long parley could we obtain a sheep. The fact is, that the ground does not lend itself to cultivation, and scarcely more to cattle-rearing. It is very marshy in places, and in the huge prairies, which stretch for 35 miles in front of the settlement, lakes appear and disappear quickly, leaving a swamp behind them. A temple near the palace does not deserve any description.

The frontier between the States of Wangtse and Wuchin lies 7 miles to the south. It is marked only by a little tent pitched on the sand. Huts of some description are noticeable in this part of the country, for the Mongols, being no longer nomads, do not feel bound to raise felt tents and wooden stakes, which always admit the cold wind in winter; they prefer the mud cottage, but have given it the sugar-loaf shape of their former tents, so as to keep up the immemorial customs, which would be upset by a rectangular room. Some of the polite customs of the Mongols are worth mentioning.

To begin with, the visitor who crosses the wooden threshold must not put his foot on it, which is a great breach of good manners. He must not bring his riding-whip with him, but must leave it with the man who holds his horse, or fasten it to the saddle, if he is alone. It would be very bad manners to pass in front of the altar which stands inside the tent on the north-west, the door being always on the south, or to put down any burden before the little statues of Buddha which usually adorn it. A well brought up Mongol will never lay the ashes of his pipe on those of the cooking hearth, and will never turn his back to the altar while speaking.

On the 24th August, before reaching the temple of Tara lama, we had occasion once again to admire the splendid stupidity of the Mongols, and the absolute faith which they have in their lamas. Having noticed a horse tied by the tail to the door of a tent, I asked why the animal was not fastened with a halter like his fellows. I was told that an old man lived here who was very ill, and finding himself worse, had sent for a lama from the Tara monastery to obtain medical advice. The unscrupulous lama had said that the old Mongol would certainly be cured if he paid a certain sum of money, and held in his hands for a whole day a rope tied to the tail of a sacred horse. The monastery always keeps a few such horses for similar occasions. Absurdities like this are not at all uncommon, and I could give plenty of other instances.

The monastery of Tara lama, which provides a peaceful life for a hundred lamas, is very dilapidated. The first of the temples of which it is composed is surrounded by dirty and ragged tents. The lamas do not seem gifted with a high order of intelligence. I could not get from them the slightest information as to the distance which lay between us and the Palace of Wuchin. Some said that it was at least 150 *lis* off, others 400. To add to the general confusion, a Chinese travelling merchant, who was trying to sell some nicknacks, and especially match-boxes, to the priests of the temple, told us as a fact that it was 300.

We set out again in overpowering heat, so severe that some of our camels, having managed to undo the rope, which, passing through their noses, tied them to the animals in front, dug up the hot sand with the nails of their feet, and squatted on the cooler ground which they thus exposed. We were crossing a country of the true desert type. Ridges of white sand succeeded one another, varied occasionally by a clump of tamarisks. The few tents which we saw were surrounded by broken boughs, which made them look like negro huts. But the country gradually improved, and we finished our march on a grassy road between high hedges, which seemed at times to be crossing an old deserted park. Here and there the men of our escort stopped to gather a small, white, wild berry, of a very bitter taste, or to pick for their evening meal a herb which smelt, unfortunately, very like garlic.

All this sand was extremely tiring to the horses, and though our camels were quite at home in it, our steeds were exhausted, when we met the troops of Mandarins and soldiers whom the

King of Wuchin, the actual chief of the Ordos Confederation, had sent to meet us.

Having decided to give us the best reception possible, the King was awaiting us under a great umbrella of yellow silk, surrounded by his Ministers and the chief lamas of the country. When we arrived all those who accompanied us broke into a mad gallop, amidst a deafening noise of crackers. After a ceremonious introduction, the Prince himself led us to the apartment reserved for us, and soon after I called upon him, following the most exact rules of diplomacy. He was not a very interesting person, but I had an opportunity of observing the great lama of the Ordos, who had been recommended to me as a man of superior intelligence. Of middle age, and corpulent appearance, his face was attractive and refined. He wore on his yellow hat a button of the same kind and degree as that of the Prince, but was dressed in purple. The people undoubtedly showed more respect to him than to the Prince. He always lives with the chief of the Confederation, and is the undisputed head of the temples scattered over the Ordos. Entirely independent of Lhasa and Kumbum, he maintains fairly constant relations with these two sacred cities by means of the pilgrimages which he organises from time to time.

Like all similar dignitaries, he tries to exaggerate his importance, and, in answer to one of my questions, assured me that he had a million lamas under him. He has quite twenty thousand, and is supposed to be very hostile to Europeans; but I think he is only hostile to the missionaries who are working directly against him. On the other hand, his quick intelligence is inclined towards progress, and he did not rest until I had explained to him the working of telegraphs, telephones, and railways, of which he had heard.

We decided, on the day after our arrival in the kingdom, to go to an antelope hunt. These graceful animals wander in the neighbourhood in herds of from three to five hundred. We succeeded in bringing down three. One of them, which was only wounded, cried and wept like a human being, until it was given the *coup de grace.*

We received the same day two ponies and a dog as presents, in return for which I gave His Majesty, to his great delight, a small nickel-plated revolver. I was, of course, careful not to add any cartridges, for fear the Prince, in his exuberant joy, might kill one of his followers, or himself. These ponies were very small like all in the Ordos, but their perfect forms, their spirit, and endurance make them remarkable animals. One may often see a Mongol load one of these animals, about twelve hands high, with a saddle weighing twenty pounds, and baggage weighing fifty, and then mount the little beast, and start on a thirty or forty days' journey across country where the grass often fails.

I note, in passing, that I could not find one of the lakes marked on the maps. The maps, printed in Germany, have been copied from ancient Chinese documents, which are often very inaccurate, and contain erroneous details. The lake possibly existed some hundreds of years ago, and has disappeared as others shortly will.

Leaving this hospitable Prince, we set out again through sand and grass plains in constant succession, and in a temperature moderated only by storms occurring regularly every three days, as I have already said. Wild animals haunt the neighbourhood, and we found the tracks of a panther near the carcass of a camel killed the day before. Accordingly I ordered my men to keep a good watch over the animals at night, but those who know the Chinese peasants will not be surprised to hear that in making my usual round towards one o'clock in the morning, I found my men huddled together in a tent trembling with fear. The panthers gave no sign of life to our great disappointment; but they must be numerous in this district, for, on one day's march, I counted more than ten carcasses of their victims.

On 22nd August we passed along a salt lake called Reulbadgi-nor, and entered a country rich in flocks, the inhabitants of which, subjects of the King of Ottock, make profit by rearing camels.

Before arriving at Ning-hsia, we only had to visit the Prince of Ottock, whose small *yamen* is on the side of a bare hill. This young Prince is but eight years old. His father and mother died four years ago of an infectious disease, probably small-pox, which thins the ranks of the Mongols, and left him to the care of his Prime Minister. The latter brought the little Prince to see us, with his face washed—no doubt for the first time. The cleaning process had only been superficial, and a fine black line made a natural necklace round his neck. I presented him with a musical box, and in return he gave me a splendid grey roan stallion, and a pistol, which I have managed to preserve through many difficulties.

He also ordered his soldiers to drill before us, and to fire their primitive guns. It was a remarkably grotesque sight. Lead being very rare in the wild country of Ottock, the veterans loaded their weapons with small pebbles, and one of them burnt his face by neglecting the elementary precaution of turning his head away when the powder caught fire and the shot left the gun. Nobody cared in what direction the bullets, or rather the pebbles, went. The Prime Minister told me with pride that his master could lead to battle six thousand soldiers as brave as these, commanded by eighty-five captains with blue, and nineteen generals with red coral buttons.

Poor little Prince, he lives alone in his narrow palace surrounded by sacred books, in which he is instructed by toothless old masters. Never the least distraction, never a game, never a laugh.

Even his brothers have been removed from him, for his tutors believe that his childhood must be a serious one, that he may learn to rule over some thousands of shepherds scattered in this corner of the world.

We soon came in sight of the summits of the mighty range of Alashan, which begins at Ning-hsia, and finally loses itself in the sands of the desert, west of the Yellow River. After a few more days' march over the undulating plain of dry grass, we reached this prefectoral city in the Province of Kansu. Not far away, the Great Wall runs along the river Ara-cha-gol, and the Ordos Desert terminates at the foot of its ruins. We had crossed it without any difficulty, caused either by Nature or by man.

CHAPTER III

BURIED CITIES OF ALASHAN

HAVING crossed the Great Wall and the river Ara-cha-gol we were no longer in the Ordos, but still had to cover a small distance to reach Ning-hsia. Above all we still had to cross the Yellow River. Although the day was well advanced, we decided to make a great effort to reach that prefecture before nightfall. But we had not allowed for a series of incidents which delayed us. To begin with, we had to wait awhile at the gates of the little town of Hong-chong-ku. Although very dismal to look at and seeming practically deserted, it still gloried in the presence of three or four Mandarins. The circuit of its walls was nearly empty, the old inhabitants had all emigrated in the hope of finding more fertile lands, but the force of custom is so strong in China, that a sub-prefect of the third grade was still kept there by the Government.

An excellent man was this sub-prefect. He offered us delicious peaches grown in Kansu, and seemed very anxious to see us start again for Ning-hsia. He no doubt had no desire to disburse

THE GREAT WALL. AT A POINT 2,000 MILES FROM PEKIN.

[To face p. 52.

the few *sapeques* that a halt for the night on our part would have cost him. He insisted on accompanying us to the boat which he had prepared for us on hearing of our arrival, and I must admit that I never saw a Mandarin exert himself to such an extent. He ran in all directions, shouting and gesticulating, giving such preposterous orders that it took us more than an hour to put on board the little luggage that we wished to have with us on reaching Ning-hsia. The over-tired camels were to follow on the next day.

The crossing of the river presented no difficulty, but the landing on a strip of slippery mud caused a few harmless tumbles, and as I was ordering my men to start at once, we observed that the soldier given us by the sub-prefect to act as a guide had deserted, taking advantage of the gathering darkness. This occurrence was exceedingly disagreeable. From our starting-point a great number of roads branched off in all directions. We could not guess as to which would lead us quickest to our goal, and I had to trust to chance to direct our steps. Chance proved no friend to the weary traveller, for it was nearly two o'clock in the morning when we reached the wooden shutters studded with huge nails, which formed the gates of the great town. We were very tired, having travelled since six o'clock on the previous morning, and our mounts trembled on their exhausted legs.

Following track after track we had covered a long way from the Yellow River in the dark, and had been badly received at the few houses of the rustics from whom we enquired the way. The traveller who knocks at a door at unreasonable hours is naturally taken for an evil-doer, and is more likely to be bitten by a raging watch-dog than to gather any useful directions. Even on reaching the city gates our bad luck was not over. Probably stupefied with opium the guardians of this noble citadel slept a sleep that the most alarming shouts and piercing cries could not disturb. At last, after we had waited nearly half an hour a night watchman came to find out the cause of this extraordinary disturbance, and without answering his question, as soon as he opened the door, we burst into the town like a whirlwind.

The rest of the night we spent in a disgusting hotel, thickly peopled with undesirable inhabitants. Our first care on the following morning was to establish ourselves in the inn reserved for touring Mandarins. The prefect sent some of his satellites to hang up lanterns made of red cloth over our door, and we set out to inspect the town.

It is only moderately interesting. Having reached the terrace of an old temple which rises in the heart of this ancient city, we discovered that misery and ruin held undisputed sway everywhere. Hardly a quarter of the whole enclosure is inhabited. The rest is given up to swamps, heaps of verdure, and waste land. However, some remaining ruins here and there point to greater prosperity in the past. Opium has largely killed this city, all of whose inhabitants indulge in this drug, and when once this awful vice has thoroughly mastered a Chinaman, he sells all he has—his land, his wives and children, the roof, doors, and windows of his house, in summer nearly all his clothing, and dies of cold in winter, stripped and naked in the street.

Commerce has consequently diminished considerably. Nowadays nearly all that the Mongols buy comes from Kwei-hua-cheng and Pao-tu, a very commercial city on the Yellow River to the west, and about 180 miles from the Blue Town. While at Pao-tu the chief firms are worth 100,000 *taels*, those at Ning-hsia do not reach in value the sum of 20,000. Ning-hsia practically exists on the corn trade, wool, camels' hair, and the manufacture of excellent carpets of all hues and sizes, from a saddle-cloth to the covering of the largest Krang. The dues paid by the boats that carry from Kansu to Kwei-hua-cheng the produce of this great province, bring in a large and valuable profit to the Mandarins, but very little to the general population.

Having left the old temple behind us and crossed the relics of fortifications which lie in the centre of the city, we went towards two very high towers in excellent preservation, which are the only monuments really worthy of attention. They are about 125 feet high, and have seven stories. It is absolutely forbidden to climb the stairs within, since the day when a merchant, having mounted to the top storey, threw himself down and dashed out his brains. Never having succumbed to the fascination of climbing stairs, several hundred steps high, we did not insist upon admission. But the view from the top of these towers should be very fine, for it must command the plains of the Ordos, the great ribband of the Yellow River, and the mountains of Alashan. These mountains rise on the west and north-west not far from Ning-hsia. Their highest altitude is only 10,500 feet, but I doubt if there is anywhere a mountain chain more bare, uncultivated, and wild. I shall allude to this again later on.

Having returned to the inn we presided at a distribution of small gifts for the recompense of the Chinese and Mongol Mandarins who had accompanied us across the Ordos. The presents, which consisted chiefly of pieces of silk, saddles, pipes, and snuff-boxes, were received by the Chinese with expressions of the liveliest gratitude. But not so by the Mongol Mandarins. Being very poor, the highest do not blush to accept small pieces of money, and our gifts in kind did not seem to please them. I acted however, as though I did not understand the mimic farce of their troubled faces, and I dismissed the whole crowd with a few words of good-will. I learnt later that the Mongols promptly resorted to the nearest shops and sold for a quarter of their value the presents they had received. With the proceeds of the sale they proceeded to buy Chinese brandy, and became so intoxicated that they could not start on their homeward way for two or three days.

When a Mongol gets the chance of eating his fill at some one else's expense he can take in more nourishment than a member of any other race. During the two days that I entertained the King of Ottock's servants at Ning-hsia they ate 60 lbs. of flour, without counting other ingredients, being only eight men in all. Poor fellows! after all, I don't blame them, for they often spend days practically fasting.

Towards evening the Tchentai, or Commander-in-Chief of the district, came to visit us. This exalted officer had not been with us more than five minutes, drinking the cup of tea, with which, according to etiquette, I had at once supplied him, when I perceived that he was particularly uncomfortable. His manners were constrained, and his politeness forced. I questioned him closely, anxious to discover the reason of his strange behaviour, and soon found that he had divers disagreeable affairs and complications on his mind, which had recently arisen between the authorities and the Christian Missions of San-tao-ho and the neighbourhood. He told me a series of more or less unlikely stories, but amongst them some facts which seemed unluckily only too probable. The most recent disorder was due to concessions of land, and blood had been shed.

I do not intend at present to enlarge upon the subject of missionaries and missions, of their methods of work, of the good and the evil which they bring about, but I will merely state that their custom of setting up and establishing colonies of Christian peasants, and trying to withdraw them more or less from the control of their natural governors, however vicious the latter may be, is one of the reasons which make a good understanding impossible between the missionaries and the Mandarins. Soon after this description of the situation the Tchentai rose and went off to smoke a large number of pipes of opium in his dilapidated palace. Several other important people also came to see us, but all seemed more or less inimical and averse to us, and realising that we could expect no good from them we decided to lose no time in leaving Ning-hsia.

Our way lay northward and followed, at a greater or less distance, the course of the Yellow River. The road was dusty, flat, and dull. As our animals were still tired after crossing the Ordos, we moved only slowly through a monotonous country; on all sides were flourishing crops, for the plain is alluvial, formed by the river, and exceedingly fertile. The cottages, as usual, were made of mud without any taste or ornament. Here and there popular superstition had erected a small temple to the genii of all kinds, which the imagination of that childish people has created. These pagodas are generally crumbling to ruin, and keep only some strips of painting, constantly rain-washed, as evidence of their former glories. The irrigation of the fields was well devised, and the channels had been dug with a genuine knowledge of the requirements of cultivation.

We went slowly through some small villages where our presence excited public curiosity, and we stopped for the night at an inn where a strong smell of opium prevailed in spite of our care in opening both doors and windows. The following morning the cold was intense as compared with the day before, with a cutting north wind blowing from the already ice-covered plain of the Upper Gobi. Our march was consequently a trying one, and we were glad to reach Ping-lo, and to fall upon a hot meal offered us by an obliging shopkeeper, who gave us hospitality for some hours. Ping-lo has been a flourishing city, but here, as in all northern China, half the town is in ruins. Everywhere it is the same true and sorrowful story of a nation that has ruined itself by its vices and stagnation.

Travelling as fast as the condition of our steeds would allow, we succeeded in reaching the mission of Hia-hin-tse before night. The road, fairly good to start with, became more difficult as we advanced along the great canal which was dug by the Jesuits before their great exodus from China more than two centuries ago. This canal was made with great skill, for after this long lapse of time, the water which still flows along it has done very little damage to its banks. It distributes its fertilising fluid over regions which, but for it, would be almost wholly barren, being a little above the level of the inundations of the river.

Having left the canal the road became very bad. As the river had flooded the high road we had to turn off across wheat fields, often flooded as well. We used the hedges between the fields and the tracks trodden by the cattle. The result of all these inconveniences was that we reached Hia-hin-tse very late in the evening. The scenery before us at dawn next morning was both depressing and strange, but one not easily forgotten.

On three sides a sheet of water poured out by the Yellow River stretched calm and mighty. It had covered the fields, overthrown the houses, flooded the roads, and, to put it shortly, arrested all life. On its waters, hardly stirred by a light wind, flotsam of all kinds was to be seen, a testimony to the wretchedness of the inhabitants, driven from their homes by the pitiless flood. Here were the beams of a roof, there a coffin. The current, in some places, fairly swift, especially where it had burst the river banks, had been strong enough to detach several of these funereal objects from their resting-places, and those that had not been entirely submerged floated half rotting on the surface, sometimes containing the relics of skeletons. The custom of the poor Chinese of depositing coffins upon the fields, without even covering them with earth, leaves them open to these mischances. In some places where the level of the flood had begun to sink, amid fragments of wood and rags of cloth, one struck one's foot against a bleached skull half full of water.

On the chief road leading to the main entrance of the mission, and a little to the right, rose a funereal structure several feet high, made of a rope fixed to two stakes of wood. Cases, with bars far apart, ten in number, swung from this rope in the wind, and held no less than ten heads of executed criminals. Some months before Hia-hin-tse had been the scene of a tragic murder of missionaries in the following circumstances.

During the trouble of 1900 the wives of some Christian Chinese had been seized, and sold in all directions. Several of them had been bought by Mussulmans, who are numerous and powerful in this district. The missionaries, eagerly seeking for these women wherever they were to be found, and rescuing them without paying the indemnity demanded by their actual husbands, had raised against themselves lively feelings of hatred and revenge. A coalition was formed which resulted in a plot and the consequent slaughter of two Belgian priests. The Mandarins on hearing of this had arrested a certain number of supposed criminals, and had beheaded them. To make the punishment better known, and to produce a greater effect upon the people, they had suspended these hideous trophies close to the scene of this crime, and, moreover, as the Mussulmans were far from being pacified, and the agitation continued, they had stationed at Hia-hin-tse a small picket of soldiers with instructions to keep order. These gentlemen spent their time in smoking opium and in plundering the surrounding peasantry, and if fresh trouble breaks out in this spot, I shall be surprised if these soldiers do not take the lead in any crime that may be committed.

Having enjoyed the kind hospitality offered us for three days, we resumed our journey to San-tao-ho, the most important of the Christian colonies established in Mongolia, which I was very anxious to see. To do so, San-tao-ho being some hundreds of miles down the Yellow River to the north, we had only to follow the banks of the river. However, this course, though simple, did not attract us, for not far from Hia-hin-tse great sand-banks come down to the level of the water, and being very loose, make a march over them very difficult.

On the suggestion of a native we decided to make for Shih-tsui-tse, close by, and to hire a boat there, and go down the swift current to our destination. No sooner decided than done; we did not linger. We reached the little town of Shih-tsui-tse, at 5 P.M., as we had been long delayed on our road by diverse sections of the flood, and by the slippery mud left behind by the receding waters. It is only a tiny village, and but for the constant passage of boats would not even exist.

The boat which had been reserved for us was about 30 feet long, and something like 10 feet broad. It was flat bottomed and square prowed, divided into three compartments by wooden screens. In the middle compartment a kind of hut of matting had been constructed in which we settled ourselves very comfortably, delighted by the idea of drifting lazily down the stream, and of avoiding a ride of several miles on horse-back with the north wind blowing in our faces.

We did not leave that night, the darkness being too dense, but the master of the boat, a suspicious-looking Mussulman, wearing the little white cap peculiar to his race, assured us that he would start down stream at daybreak next morning. On waking we found that he had kept his word. We were gliding rapidly on the muddy waters between the wide banks of the river. The appearance of the country was constantly changing. First bare and naked rocks, then bushes of tamarisk, then sand-hills shining in the sun. The boat went down the current almost as fast as the stream, and I calculated our pace at about 8 miles an hour when the banks drew together, and at about 5 when they opened out again. Nothing could be more pleasant than this rapid and peaceful motion without dust or friction. After many months this journey is one of our most agreeable recollections. The country that we were slipping through was lighted up by a warm sun, and the creaking of the long piece of wood acting as a rudder was the only noise that reached our ears.

From time to time we passed a barge very low in the water, its speed checked by its heavy load; or we met an empty boat returning from Pao-tu painfully towed along the banks by the boatmen.

From Shih-tsui-tse, where we had embarked, to Pao-tu, the hire of a boat is 50 *taels*, and a boat carries 30 *tins* of merchandise, or 9,000 lbs. in Chinese measure. A boat accomplishes the journey of 300 miles in six or seven days, but to get up stream again and return to its starting-point it requires three or four weeks, according to the energy of its crew. A large number of boats ply upon this river. Between the two points which I have named, and between which I could gather statistics, no less than 5,000 boats ply their trade. A service of steam tugs to tow them to and fro, and reduce the trip from thirty-five days to six, would meet with certain success, and would unquestionably fill the pockets of its shareholders. The river is nowhere too swift for navigation or too shallow for the boats. Our crew repeatedly assured me that the river was at least 5 feet deep all over its course from bank to bank; that depth is ample. There are certainly constantly shifting sand-banks, but it is the business of the pilots to locate their positions daily, and to avoid them.

CAMP IN THE DESERT.

[To face p. 64.

On the afternoon of this restful and charming day, while we were gliding along the range of mountains called Arbas-ulan, about 7,000 feet in height, the most important elevation on the Ordos plateau, I suddenly sighted an antelope drinking in fancied security, and betraying no excitement at our passing. In the hope of getting a good shot I gave orders to draw near the bank, and set about getting possession of the precious game. I soon saw that it had left the water and was browsing on the tough grass. I fired, the animal gave a leap, trotted a few yards, and stopped. I had obviously missed it, and expected to see it disappear at full speed, but to my great surprise it did not move. With a grateful uplifting of my heart I aimed at it again, and brought it down. However, I was covered with confusion and horror on discovering when I reached it that the graceful animal's neck was decked with the prayer-slips and bits of red cloth with which the superstitious Mongols dedicate all sorts of beasts to the gods, and was in fact a tame one!

Not far away towards the mountains I was soon aware of two tents, and of a still more disagreeable sight, namely, some half dozen Mongols running up gesticulating wildly. With the help of two boatmen who had followed me, I tried in all haste to carry the antelope to the boat. But the Mongols were too fast for us, they cut across our path, and began to insult and threaten us. To calm them I offered them an ingot of silver, but that was not enough for them. They demanded a sum which it would have been quite absurd to pay. Handing them 5 *taels*, about three times the value of the antelope at Ning-hsia, I made for the boat and got on board safely with my booty, which proved afterwards to be very tender and tasty.

In the evening we stopped at the village of Tung-ku on the bank of the river, for the boats never continue their journey at night. This is a little *point perdu*, half buried in sand, which the wind piles up in mounds for some distance, and owes its relative importance only to the salt trade.

After a peaceful night we continued our journey through country very like that which we had seen the day before. On the left bank were numerous tamarisks and sand-hills, on the right bank sand and dry mud. Towards three o'clock in the afternoon we came in sight of San-tao-ho, and having found with some difficulty a convenient landing-place, we were heartily welcomed by Monsignor Bermyn, Vicar Apostolic of the Ordos and of Western Mongolia. As I have said before San-tao-ho is one of the largest Christian colonies to be met with, and one of the most flourishing. Thousands of peasants live around it, and though I do not approve of the principles by which they have been collected, yet I must admire the hard work and the perseverance displayed by the missionaries who have erected such an establishment.

Here, as everywhere, at the same season of the year, the flood had done great damage. The disaster now extended so far that most of the crops were destroyed, and the cultivators were compelled to live on little, and to look to the mission as a nursing mother. San-tao-ho, properly speaking, comprises a fairly large quadrangular circuit of walls built of mud mixed with straw, supporting a raised walk. These walls offer a good resistance to bullets and common balls. My own experience enables me to state that a Mannlicher rifle bullet fired from 20 yards off does not penetrate them further than 6 inches. Their greatest enemy is the water from the floods which washes their base, and dislodges little by little the material of which they are built.

Inside, the church, the residence, a large garden and a small village are side by side. Also the dwellings of the missionaries, who had given us one of their best rooms, are comfortable, what gave us the keenest pleasure were the vegetable garden and the park, with its large and fine trees. Such splendour surpasses the expectation of the traveller who has just crossed the Ordos, and pauses for a moment at the entrance to the terrible desert of Alashan.

San-tao-ho has a history of its own, which it would take a long time to record in detail. I will only say that during the troubles of 1900, instead of running away and leaving their Christians in the moment of danger, after giving them many fine promises in times of peace, as certain misguided missionaries did, the missionaries of San-tao-ho undertook a fine defence, which was rewarded by the flight of the Boxers and the safety of their converts.

Around San-tao-ho there are numerous Christians cultivating the lands conceded to them, and living happily enough together. When there is any dispute, or any cause for the intervention of authority, it is referred to the bishop, who maintains a constant court of appeal. The worst of this system is that the Christians consider their missionaries morally bound to support them under all circumstances, whether they are right or wrong. In case of famine, instead of looking for work or relying on their own industry for their food, they have recourse to the ever-open purse. Under these conditions to be a Christian is to be practically certain of support. It is not to be wondered at that many find in a change of religion a provision for daily bread.

The authorities are apparently very ill-disposed towards San-tao-ho. I had proofs of that at Ning-hsia. Here I gained more. Pamphlets, hostile to Europeans, have been posted up close by. In fact San-tao-ho is perpetually at war with all the neighbouring authorities. The actions of the Tartar Marshal do not make for peace, when he takes back from the actual tenants the lands yielded on bail by the Mongols. In doing this he acts in the name of Pekin, but, by offering no reasonable compensation, he unduly irritates the people. Bands of brigands scour the country, and are largely composed of dispossessed persons. One frequently hears of murders committed upon the official envoys or their troops. The authority of the Tartar Marshal does not seem to be worth much here.

I mention all these little facts to give the reader as exact an idea as possible of what is going on away from the great centres. At Pekin the pass word is "Set fair"; in the interior it is otherwise. Jealousy, lying, treason, and murder occur daily, whether between Christians and Chinese or among the Chinese themselves. It has always been so; it will be so for years to come, wherever the influence of Japan does not extend. We hear on all sides that China is changing. China has not changed. It is only her Government that is trying to change. In certain directions it may succeed, but a long number of years that no one can calculate must pass before the hundreds of millions of Chinese peasants shall awake from the senseless lethargy of their daily life.

We decided to leave our hospitable shelter for some days in order to push on a little into the north of Alashan. We wished to visit the old buried cities which used to flourish on the banks now deserted by the Yellow River. The river has often changed its course, being constantly divided by the sands of the desert. We also intended to visit, on our way from the south, the temple of Aque-miao, at which the Russian explorer, Obrotchieff, spent some time on his way from the north-west.

The caravan was made up of camels. I had bought some new ones, and had no idea of taking any other animals into a country largely composed of loose sand.

An amusing incident marked the beginning of our march. One camel, awkward as they all are, managed to tumble into a ditch of thick mud between the road and a wheat field. When once fallen a camel can only get up again if it can arrange its large feet conveniently under it, and if the ground is nearly flat. In this case it was not so. And the animal lay with all 4 feet in the air, perfectly resigned, and incapable of a single movement to help itself. To draw it out took more than half an hour, and required the united efforts of many men, with cords passed under the camel's back.

Having marched 35 *lis*, say 11 miles, to the north of San-tao-ho, across the fields of the Christians we turned certainly westward, and at once entered upon a change of scene. When we had crossed two or three sand-hills we were in open desert. We followed a faint path made by caravans of camels which had gone before us, and that evening we halted on the edge of a well with no margin, imperceptible from 10 yards away.

The following morning we started early, and did 13 miles in the same direction before breakfast. As all this country is simply a desert, with very few wells dug by caravan drivers, we did not find any water to drink, and started again at once. Towards evening we reached the bank of one of the old beds of the Yellow River. The wind has made enormous fissures in the bank, and all the neighbourhood has suffered from this erosion. Not far away, there is a well, sheltered by two sand-hills, which could not be found without a skilled guide, such as the Mongol Norbo whom we had brought with us. The mountains were covered by clouds, all the sand-hills were alike, and yet this son of the desert did not hesitate for a moment about the actual position of the well which he had only visited himself once before.

On 16th September we only travelled a short distance towards the south-west, but we reached a particularly interesting point of the desert. Amid the bare and wild expanse were more than three hundred tombs, half sunk in the alluvial ground, some covered with sand, somc gaping, others perfectly intact. These are the most striking and impressive traces of a former considerable civilisation which we were the first to look upon, after a lapse of time impossible to calculate accurately, during which they have been lost to the knowledge of men.

These tombs are from three to four yards long

and, as a rule, a yard and a half wide. There are generally two together, and round each of these pairs the old lines of the ditches which surrounded them can be traced. This is the usual Chinese procedure in the case of the tombs of rich persons. A ditch or a low wall divides them from the neighbouring field. Their summits are in the shape of a dome; the space which they occupy is rectangular. They are built of large and heavy bricks, grey in colour, occasionally red, and about a foot square. Some of these bricks have been reduced to powder by the wind and the sand, but some are still perfectly intact, and they are certainly the heaviest and strongest bricks that I have ever seen.

I had decided to extract from these tombs all the information I could, and I ordered the men to attack one of the best preserved with a pickaxe. I had some trouble in getting this done, for to a Chinamen the violation of a tomb is a serious matter, and he fully believes in his superstition that such an act will cast an evil spell over the rest of his life.

However, after some time they had to obey, and the pickaxe resounded on these old bricks, which offered a great resistance. Having removed the upper part of the tomb we found a piece of exceedingly hard ground exactly filling the interior. The men dug a kind of well 5 or 6 feet deep, and from this depth the spade brought up a large quantity of broken wood. This wood, which seemed to me to be poplar, must have been very ancient. The fragments were, moreover, scattered and separated by layers of earth. I was quite unable to find bones or any other object. Leaving my men to cook their dinner, I went down myself into the hole that they had dug to examine the ground more closely. It was alluvial ground which did not seem to have been placed here by human hand, for every three or four millimetres an unbroken horizontal line ran across the deposit. This alluvial earth seemed to have penetrated the tomb, and settled there long after the construction of the monument.

Not far from the tombs, and spread in great abundance over the ground, were small fragments of pottery. Having found only the remains of ancient coffins inside the tombs, I set myself to search carefully in the places where I found this pottery, and was lucky enough to find some old coins, ancient *sapeques*, arrow heads in flint, and the handle of a kind of spoon. Amongst all these fragments I selected several broken pieces of pottery which had formerly been part of vases and basins, the design on which was specially remarkable. I found also some earthenware marbles such as children play with, a whetstone for sharpening knives, and various objects more or less broken up, of which I could not determine the origin or the use.

Continuing my investigation I came to an old brick furnace entirely demolished. Was it that in which the builders of the tombs used to make the magnificent bricks that we had admired? I could not be sure, but it was likely enough. Then again the ground was covered with pottery broken almost to dust. I could not understand how it had become reduced to such tiny fragments. How did it happen that they were hardly covered with earth, and seemed to have lain there only a few weeks? Probably the wind had recently displaced the sand which covered them. However, night came on, and I had to postpone my researches till the next day.

At dawn, on 17th September, I began again to examine the traces of this vanished life. On the west, amid fairly high sand-hills, I found a great number of human bones. Having examined them carefully I discovered that they were not of great antiquity, and were only the skeletons of Mongols abandoned at this deserted spot, according to their custom, by their relations after death.

As a more prolonged search did not seem likely to bring any fresh results, we marched back towards the well which we had left the evening before, to the great pleasure of our horses, who had had nothing to drink for more than twenty-four hours. There is not a drop of water or a patch of good grass in all this place.

The night of the 18th September was very cold, 24° F. We suffered from it only less than our people, who believing that winter would not set in so soon, were still wearing their light

GRAVES DISCOVERED NEAR POU-HOTO.

[To face p. 74.

summer clothing. They spent the night in feeding a great fire with dry brushwood, and did not sleep at all, so that they were ready to make an early start.

Moving northward again, through a desolate and dreary desert, we made for some ruins, the exact situation of which our guide Norbo said that he knew. The Mongols, who venture into these regions in pursuit of a strayed camel, call these ruins Poro-hoto or Grey Town.

Having journeyed for 20 miles, and crossed an old bed of the Yellow River, we stopped in a kind of funnel formed by the wind, between three high sand-hills, which sheltered us from the cold wind. The camels began to eat some brushwood round about. All was silent and still.

The ruined city was not far from our camp, and we went there the next morning accompanied by ten men carrying pickaxes and spades.

This city is rectangular in form with four gates, and in one of the angles there was clearly a citadel, behind which there were two temples. On the ground are remains of tiles from the roof, and many pieces of iron and lead which seemed to have been melted in a great fire. I began to dig here; the men worked willingly, for this time we were not profaning a tomb. My disappointment grew with the size of the hole that we made. The spade brought up nothing but fragments like those upon the surface—bits of iron, lead, or leather, and pieces of coloured tiles. I had another opening made a little further on. The result was the same, except that we found a coin such as we had found two days before in the tomb. I therefore gave up the site of the temples, and we went round the circuit of the city. Large stones without cement unquestionably mark the site of the *yamen* built against the northern wall and facing south, in front of the chief gate. These stones were foundations of the different buildings, and from them the fallen rooms can be reconstructed; on all sides there were many coloured tiles which had crumbled away, and fragments which seemed to have been wantonly broken.

As we were finishing this identification a Mongol appeared in a breach of the circuit wall, and politely enquired the object of our visit. When satisfied on this matter he told us that no Mongol in Alashan knows the true origin and history of Poro-hoto. Long before our visit the shepherds and camel drivers, who happened to pass close to the site, had searched carefully and taken all the coins and small objects which they found on the surface of the ground. He assured us that not far from our camp there were more tombs, and according to legends the bones inside them were much larger and heavier than those of the men of to-day. Having thanked this good Mongol, who lived in a poor little tent some miles to the north, and made a living by rearing some thin camels, we made for the site of the tombs of which he had spoken. They were like those

THE RUINS OF THE TOWN OF POU-HOTO, ALASHAN.

[To face p. 76.

which we had examined two days before, but in a better state of preservation. I managed to unearth a thighbone, but its length was quite normal, and it did not seem very ancient.

Towards six o'clock in the evening, after having sent our guide Norbo to buy provisions from a Mongol tent, we began our march towards a well which the Mongol had told us was not far away, and which I hoped to find myself. Far away or not, I could not find it, and after having wandered till ten o'clock without a guide, and following constantly crossing trails of camels, I finally ordered a halt in a little valley between the sand-hills, which had the advantage of being covered with brushwood, which afforded the means of making a fire, and that was something. We had not a drop of water, and after a day spent in pretty severe exertion in the ruins of Poro-hoto, not having had anything to drink since morning, we were very thirsty. So keen was our need for water that we could not eat some rapidly roasted meat, which would only have increased our thirst.

We lay down to sleep, after having heard the complaints of the men in the caravan. Whenever anything disagreeable happens, these gentlemen, who are accustomed to very little, are loudest in their lamentations.

On 20th September the sun had hardly risen when we set out in the hope of quenching our thirst as soon as possible. Under the friendly light of day we could follow the wide road without losing it, and having at last found a trail made by caravan camels, and not wandering animals, I knew that we should soon find a well.

As we advanced, the sand-hills became higher and broader, and there were very few traces of vegetation. We moved fast, and the mountains which sheltered Aque-miao drew nearer to us. Suddenly from the top of a sand-hill we saw two or three hundred camels driven by some Mongol girls, making for a point not far on our left. Accordingly we changed our course a little, and came to a well where these girls were watering the camels, which are brought up in freedom in the district. These girls were about sixteen or seventeen years old, and had smiling faces, clouded for a moment by the surprise caused by our arrival. They did not seem frightened by the camels which crowded around them, biting and rearing in the hope of getting the first drink. From time to time they struck them on the nose with a bit of rope, and went on quietly drawing water in a wooden cane bucket, as closely made as possible, but which allowed a great part of the precious liquid to escape on the way. Having asked them for a little water, they amiably offered us the bucket out of which a camel had just drunk, and were greatly astonished at our insisting upon a more appetising draught.

We made a short halt near this well, and ate

a light meal quickly cooked on a fire easily fed with camel dung.

As we were setting out again, Norbo appeared, bringing the necessary provisions. He had spent all the night, he said, looking for us, terrified by the thought that we might be lost.

I knew the Mongol well enough to be aware that all his explanations were a mere matter of politeness. Norbo had spent an excellent night not far from the well where he had rejoined us, after an excellent dinner, the proof of which was a considerable breach in the provisions which he had brought.

We were not far from the lamasery of Aque-miao, which we intended to visit. To get there we had only to cross the little strip of sandy desert 4 or 5 miles across which still lay between us and the Chara-narin-ulan mountains.

Towards noon we reached these mountains. They are not very high, and are absolutely barren. Their naked sides rise above the desert like a great deep-coloured wall, sometimes blue, sometimes yellow, or white or pink. At the foot of them, here and there, a spring or a well gives water for the caravans coming from Kansu through Rapalaraitze, and going to Pao-tu or to Urga. Small temples have been built in these places, and the lamas live on the tolls of the caravan drivers.

Before entering the Pass of Aque, named from the temple inside it, I noticed a little to the right a high and broad fissure which is called the Pass of the Kalchas. Through it many missionaries escaped in 1900, avoiding the danger which they thought was imminent in Kansu. This was also the road taken by one of the envoys sent by the King of Belgium into Kansu, in the hope of securing mining concessions. The name of the Pass of Kalchas, given it by the caravan drivers, is justified by the fact that it leads to the country of the Kalchas Mongols who live in the north of Gobi, not far from Urga.

The gorge which we had entered contained some picturesque bits, in spite, or perhaps because, of their extreme wildness. All along the river bed, which was dry, were successions of cairns, covered with small stones set up by the pious superstition of Mongol pilgrims, who believe that this homage will please the gods.

As we went up, the ravine became extremely narrow, and left us just room to pass; then suddenly it opened into a circle surrounded by hills. In this circle were the terraced Temples of Aque-miao. We reached them at 2 P.M.

The lamas had had only one European visitor, and they seemed to look upon the approach of our modest caravan with some fear. In 1900 they caused the plunder and death of Christians of San-tao-ho and the neighbouring mission, by working upon the excited feelings of the people, and preaching a holy war. They knew that we came from San-tao-ho, and dreaded

THE TEMPLE OF AQUE-MIAO.

[*To face p.* 80.

reprisals. In trepidation they led us towards the great tent adorned with festal cushions of yellow tapestry, and pitched in a court, while the caravan drivers went to another tent, rather larger but quite plain.

The usual courtesies took place, tea was poured out and drunk, and little by little I reassured them about our visit. We only wanted to see their temples, which had been described to us as very interesting, and having done that we should leave the next day. The latter portion of my speech seemed to give them peculiar pleasure, and at my request they prepared to act as guides to us.

Aque-miao was not like any of the lamaseries which we had seen. Its site is extremely wild, a little plain formed by the meeting of the valleys which open upon it, surrounded by pointed and almost inaccessible rocks, which keep the sun from it nearly all day. The temples have only one storey, they are white with square windows, painted red, and they have terraces. A great cairn rises in front of them, and the annual fair or market is held around it. The houses of the Buddhist priests cling here and there to the sides of the rocks, and one has to reach them by such difficult paths that, having once arrived safely, one has no great desire to go down again.

However the most curious sights of Aque-miao are not confined to its position, but are to be found more especially in a temple built in a grotto half-way up the hill, and in an underground passage of which the Mongols speak with the greatest veneration.

To reach the chief temple we climbed a pretty steep stair which brought us out 300 feet above the other temples. A painted wooden railing ran all the way up, and here and there, but very close together, are fixed small praying wheels, so that while going up to the temple the lamas may reap a large harvest of merit. It seems to me that the feat of climbing this slippery stair, which must be impassable after a fall of snow, several times a day, is in itself sufficiently meritorious. When we reached the gates of the temple we had to wait some time, for the porter in charge of the keys was very old, and had great difficulty in climbing. When the heavy gates were opened we made our way into a natural cave which has been utilised by the lamas, and transformed into a hall of worship. It does not contain any large or remarkable statues, but there are in it a great number of silk rags, banners, and wax candles. The hall was cold and damp, and a strong smell of grease made a longer stay unpleasant to the nostrils of a European.

When we had come down again from this eyrie I asked our guide, a very respectable lama, to judge by his girth, to take us at once to the grotto. He promised to go and fetch the key, but returned no more. I had a search made for him, but he was not to be found. As to the other lamas, when questioned, they professed a complete ignorance as to the living place of our guide, and affirmed that he alone could open the grotto. Clearly the lamas had no desire to see us profane this sacred place, but as it formed part of our plan of inspection, I sent to the chief lama to say that we should remain at Aque-miao, at his expense, until we had seen this famous grotto. This threat produced an excellent effect. Our guide reappeared, and without giving any excuse for his conduct, begged us to follow him. We went back about three-quarters of a mile along the road which we had trodden in the morning, and the lama invited us to scramble along the rocky rampart. At first sight it seemed to us impossible to venture upon those slippery stones in fur boots. I sent one of my men in front, but he soon came back saying that there was a narrow path. So we began to climb. In places the rock was so slippery that the help of my bare-footed men was most useful. This climb is really dangerous, a single slip, and we should have fallen into an abyss of some hundred feet.

At last we arrived safely at the entry of the grotto, and entered it through a little low wooden door, quite plain. There was thick darkness within. Some tallow candles burning before the little gilded figures hardly gave us light enough to guide our steps. The floor was very uneven, and the ceiling varied in height, with the disagreeable result that we were constantly knocking our heads against it. The pilgrims are obliged to crawl into a little hole 3 feet square in the middle of the passage to reach the furthest hall. The general effect is certainly strange, but not nearly so remarkable as I had hoped. On coming out we both gave a cry of surprise. We were red, absolutely red, in face, hands, and clothes! The walls of the grotto were of red ochre, which comes off at the least touch, and we had taken no precautions. We did our best to rid ourselves of this colouring, a little too gaudy for our taste, and our efforts seemed to give much pleasure to the lamas who were with us.

Just as we began to come down I noticed on one side a little above the entrance to the grotto a four-wheeled chariot resting on a small platform. The presence of this unexpected vehicle is thus explained. Some time ago, the lamas of Urga sent a statue of Buddha, with a caravan of pilgrims, in homage to Aque-miao. This statue was brought from the south of Siberia to Alashan on the chariot which we had seen, and the chariot had been sanctified by its burden. The statue is in the grotto, and the chariot outside. It is built so that the front wheels are not independent of the back wheels, which must prove inconvenient in turning. It seemed well preserved.

I wondered how it had been possible to drag such a heavy burden along the slippery rock, worn by the feet of lamas and pilgrims. It is but another proof that superstition is one of the most potent levers in the world.

Before leaving Aque-miao, on 21st September, we had an excellent meal, owing to the great number of red partridges which lived amongst the neighbouring rock. The lamas were very much scandalised at hearing the echo of shots in so sacred a place, but our fear of offending them gave way before our desire for a good dish. As it is contrary to their rules to kill anything, or to shed blood, the game, which has never been disturbed, is not at all wild. I was told that wild goats often come to drink at the monastery wells.

Our return to San-tao-ho was marked by one incident. Three of the camels, no doubt thinking that they had had too little to eat during the week, escaped one night, while their drivers, according to their custom, were fast asleep instead of watching.

The country was without variety, a vast alluvial plain crossed by ridges of sand occasionally lofty, and often crumbling, which made our advance difficult. With regard to this portion of the Alashan desert it is well to note these points. The sand is chiefly collected at the two ends, which touch the mountains and the river. At these points the altitude of the sand is considerable, while in the centre there is little sand, but loess and clay. On the other hand, I could not fix the general current of the wind in this district. The sand-hills face in every direction, and change very rapidly. I myself observed, on

17th September, that the strong wind which was then blowing for less than two hours described a complete circle of 360°. Rain falls seldom in the centre of this desert, and the twisted shape of the loess, now like an old tower, now hollowed into deep ravines, or built up in pyramids, must be due to æolian erosion, powerfully aided by the sand moved by the wind.

After some days spent in pleasant idleness at San-tao-ho we resumed our march towards the capital of the King of Alashan by a road which no European had ever taken, crossing another part of the desert of Alashan.

Our staff had undergone more changes. Since our Annamite cook had not been able to break himself off his drunken habits, but, on the contrary, had developed them to the extent of absorbing two quarts of Chinese brandy daily, and was quite incapable of working, I decided to give him enough money to take him back to Pekin. I have never heard of him since, and I doubt as to his whereabouts, for he would certainly have drunk his journey money in a very short time. But what could I do? He had really become a nuisance, and had to be suppressed.

Henceforth all our servants and camel drivers, six in number, were men from San-tao-ho—four Chinese and two Mongols. These latter had charge of the nine camels, which, with eight horses, formed the caravan.

Is it advantageous or otherwise to have

Christian servants when travelling in China? I should answer the question in the negative. The fact is that Christians, accustomed to being constantly helped and pampered by their missionaries, consider themselves specially unlucky unless they always receive the same amiable and confidential treatment. But the chief of a caravan must keep his men at a distance, and make himself respected, and this is impossible in dealing with Chinese Christians, who become insolently familiar, and discuss their orders as soon as they cease to grovel. After a few days they are discontented, and constantly threaten to report to their missionaries the cavalier treatment which they are receiving. With this nation above all others fear is the beginning of wisdom.

I should always recommend travellers to take with them heathen Chinese, not opium smokers, if possible, to pay them liberally, and to punish them mercilessly for the least fault. For money the Chinaman will go anywhere, and usually behaves well when his evil instincts are held in check by the hope of a large reward. The Christians are as great thieves as the heathen, but they are more hypocritical, and certainly more deceitful. Finally, there are opium smokers among them, as I proved later on.

We started under a bright sky; after some miles we reached a tamarisk wood on the banks of the Yellow River, which was very picturesque. The shrubs rise about 13 or 14 feet above the soil, and have a strong growth on a bed of sand and alluvial deposit. The river this year had uprooted a great number, the flood having been specially strong. Swamps formed by the overflow were full of wild duck, of which we killed many. They were very fat and very good eating, when kept for two or three days after being shot. One kind, called the Mandarin duck, whose feathers are yellow and black, and whose cry is shrill, is a little larger than the others, but its flesh is tough, and it is hardly worth shooting. There were wild geese also in great numbers, and the readers know as well as I do the worth of a wild goose when properly cooked.

We spent the night near a little ruined cottage inhabited by two old men, which serves the few travellers who go along the river from Ning-hsia to Pao-tu as an inn. Here the five soldiers whom the Mandarins had given us for a guard began to misbehave, and I had to bring them to reason by severer measures than mere words.

Profiting by the incapacity of the inn-keepers to defend their property, they stole and killed one of their sheep, and made a feast while the poor old men, fearing that the gallant warriors might take it into their heads to kill another, behaved as gently and politely as possible, but had tears in their eyes.

I think the main cause of the hatred shown

to Europeans is the type of soldier given them as an escort. If the traveller pays the innkeeper, the soldier gets hold of the latter, and extracts from him half of what he has received. The soldier levies a tribute of opium, provisions, forage, and money wherever he goes with a European, unless his employer, knowing what a rascal he has to deal with, keeps a strict watch over him. Under these conditions it is not surprising that tradesmen and innkeepers view the arrival of a traveller with disfavour, seeing that his presence will cost them more than they will gain from it.

After discharging these men we refused every kind of escort that was offered us, and we were received with smiling faces everywhere. On 30th September our road was like that of the day before, following the course of the river over grassy patches and through bushes of tamarisk. The population was very scattered, which seemed strange, for the soil was good, and the flood did not seem to have extended so far as in the neighbourhood of San-tao-ho.

We arrived at Tong-ku in a blinding sandstorm which lasted only a few minutes, and then swept across the Yellow River into the mountains of Arabas-ulan.

Tung-ku, near which we had spent a night in our boat on our way to San-tao-ho, contains no comfortable inn. So we asked hospitality from a shopkeeper who had just built a new house, ornamented on its carved woodwork with fresh painting in red and green. Unluckily, he was an opium-seller, and all the rooms were permeated with the dreadful odour of this nauseous drug. In any case it would have been difficult to sleep well. For all the inhabitants of the village, anxious to make our acquaintance, presented themselves one after another at our door. When we had had them shown out they did not admit defeat, but poking holes with their fingers in the paper of the windows, tried to get the best view obtainable of the faces and belongings of the foreign devils. I could not think of any means of ridding ourselves of this curious and disobliging crowd, until suddenly seizing a teapot full of hot tea I rushed to the door and sprinkled with tea the faces of the nearest. They recoiled, half amused and half angry, and disappeared after a short time, allowing us to proceed to undress.

The road that we took on 1st October to reach Wang-ien-fu, or Fu-ma-fu, the capital of Alashan, has never been traversed by any European, and hardly deserves to be styled a road at all. It is rather a trail beaten deep by the heavy tread of camels marching through the sand in Indian file. Here and there wells have been dug by the camel drivers, and usually near the wells one or two tents of very poor nomads are to be found concealed behind a mound. The whole of this portion of the country is genuine desert, in which only a few bushes grow, enough to sustain the frugal camel. The nomads live by rearing camels,

A CAMP IN THE ALASHAN DESERT.

[To face p. 90.

and by selling the wool of their few sheep, whose flesh is very unpalatable. This is not surprising, seeing that they have not one good tuft of grass to eat. The nomads also subsist upon a kind of cheese and curdled milk derived from these sheep.

From time to time they contrive to kill an antelope, a marvellous feat considering the bad quality of the arms they use. Their matchlock guns can only be fired by resting them on a tripod, the length of the barrel in proportion to the weakness of the butt making it impossible to raise them to the shoulder. The match when lighted takes some time to ignite the powder, and all this time the hunter must keep his eye upon the quarry. But he must alter the level of his gun if the animal moves, and when at last the shot is fired it does not always carry as far as the hunter has aimed. A good Mongol gun will carry perhaps 50 yards with force enough to kill. However, in spite of all these difficulties they attain success by craft and patience, sometimes stalking an animal for two or three days until they find it asleep.

These Mongols showed an extremity of terror on the approach of our caravan. We had nothing formidable about us, and our rifles were not even slung on our backs, but laid on the baggage, where they could not be seen.

On 2nd October, on nearing the tents and the well at Kreupa, where we intended to camp for the night, we saw men, women, and children leap on the backs of ponies already saddled, and gallop away. They left behind them an old woman, feeble in body and mind, who gazed fixedly upon us, and seemed to understand nothing. They had closed the doors of their tents as firmly as a Mongol tent door can be fastened, and had let their dogs loose to attack us. As these latter seemed fierce, and their teeth were certainly formidable, we approached armed with sticks, and forced the doors in with our shoulders, for we had to get some flour for our men.

We settled down as well as we could in the deserted tents, hoping that the owners would return, and that our Mongol camel drivers might be able to reassure them with a few fair words. But the night passed, and the time for departure arrived. Not a soul appeared, and we started off, leaving behind us in a conspicuous place in one of the tents a small ingot of silver.

That day we had a still more disagreeable experience on suddenly arriving from behind a ridge of sand at the wretched hovel of Kreupa. The inhabitants had no beasts to ride away on, but at the sight of us they fell on their knees and broke into lamentations. The women shrieked and rolled on the sand, the children gave vent to piercing yells. It was a scene of ludicrous panic. Our men, who grew annoyed at these postures and antics, wanted to fall upon the men with their fists. The two Mongols reviled their fellow-countrymen in the most energetic terms. I had hard work to re-establish order, and wondered what the Europeans at San-tao-ho could have done to create for their race such a reputation. This fear, fright, and weeping were all extraordinary. I never met with similar occurrences on my first journey three years before, or again in our recent crossing of the Ordos.

By degrees we obtained a hearing. All stood up, and in return for payment we procured some camel dung for our fires—very necessary, since the thermometer fell at night to 30°.

The next day we managed to buy a small calf from the Mongols of Man-ti-rai, and were received with less terror. The report that we were good payers, and did not ill-treat the natives, had obviously preceded us. These poor people are not ill-natured, but they are timid and suspicious. They are only like children. Their joys and sorrows are keen and soon over. A kind word wins their hearts. Failure to punish their faults makes them impertinent, for they attribute it to weakness. They do not understand kind actions, but have a keen sense of justice. However, the purchase of a calf proved our popularity, for the Mongols hardly ever sell these animals.

The scenery around had now changed somewhat. We had sand-hills of hard, instead of shifting and drifting sand, and after passing them we reached a great flat, devoid of grass, and very desolate in appearance, which stretched between two ranges of hills running from north to south.

We advanced at a fast pace on this firm ground, which gave good footing to the horses, and reached our goal early. As a rule, we accomplished 15 miles a day. It was not much, but some of the camels still felt their work under the burning sun of the Ordos and needed considerate treatment.

For two days the temperature had been trying. It passed continually from one extreme to the other. We were constantly putting on our furs, only to take them off again. Winter and summer were still waging a doubtful battle; in a few days winter would be victorious.

On 6th October we were still climbing a long gentle slope of loess, practically bare of grass. To the west, however, many camels were feeding, and there must be much brushwood in that neighbourhood. Hills, some of them of considerable height, ran from north to south. The brambles that grew on their sides made a fine blaze under the stars.

That night I performed an act of discipline, which I hoped might bear good fruit. I had absolutely forbidden the soldiers of our escort to smoke opium, for the excellent reasons that I loathe this abominable vice, and that the smell of opium is extremely disagreeable. However, in making a round of the camp towards midnight, I had no doubt that one of the men was smoking, for a strong smell was proceeding from one of the tents. I hastily caught up the flap, and found three soldiers happily enjoying the poison. Before they could recover from the astonishment caused by my appearance I seized their pipes and broke them across my knee. As to the boxes containing the opium, I dispersed their contents over the sands.

From our camp at Kou-ou-tou on 7th October we could see the range of hills running from east to west, behind which lies Fu-ma-fu. We should reach the capital easily that day. We had only 17 miles to cover, and the ground was easy. There had been a sharp frost during the night, but the sun had risen in the morning in a cloudless sky, and there being no wind the temperature was already 60° at nine o'clock.

At sunrise I had sent the *Fou-ye*, or sergeant, who commanded our small escort, with a Chinese visiting card and the passport, to inform His Majesty the King of Alashan of our arrival. Without this precaution I was none too sure of finding a lodging.

The road ran through low, bare hills. The monotony of their hue was occasionally broken by tints of red ochre caused by dried clay. Having progressed some 10 miles we noticed on our right a cairn raised on the summit of a small hill, about 350 feet high, which must command a view of the whole district. I immediately made for it, and did not regret my trouble on arriving. The view is extensive, and the cairn has been erected at the exact spot where the roads from the north, east, west, and southwest meet to form one single artery. To the north lay the huge plains which look fertile from this point, but which we know by experience only too often fail to provide sustenance for animals. To the west stretched a gently sloping dry country with lofty sand-drifts and two or three rocky heights. To the south were trees, and beyond them could be seen the city, and the view was bounded by a chain of hills running from east to west. On the east rose the formidable mountains of Alashan, with their varying colours changing from a slaty to a brick hue, and again to grey and white.

An hour later we reached Fu-ma-fu.

THE TOWN OF FU-MA-FU.

[*To face p.* 96.

CHAPTER IV

FU-MA-FU

We had hardly come in sight of the ramparts when two soldiers, wearing their uniform which had once been ornamented with black velvet, but which the misfortunes of years had reduced to a state of rags, greeted us on behalf of the Prince, and assured us that they had come to conduct us to the lodging reserved for us.

We followed them, and instead of entering the city we skirted the ramparts to the west and south, to reach the suburb where were the inns devoted to travellers and Chinese and Mongol merchants. Some of these inns are repulsively dirty. Not one is really possible for Europeans, especially if they wish to stay two or three days. However, our guides stopped and begged us to enter one of these doubtful hostels, with gestures as courteous and polite as if it had been a palace. The court was full of ragged people. Only one small room was free from the invasion of mule drivers, of whom the inn was full. This was the comfortable konkuan reserved for us by the Prince of Alashan.

Without dismounting or speaking I turned my

rein and ordered the caravan back. We went by the same way across the suburb, and made for the chief gate of the city. I intended to see the Prince himself, and thus to force him to offer us a more decent resting-place.

When we had entered the circuit of the walls we made a great sensation, still more so when we crossed the threshold of the palace without dismounting. A servant of the Prince appeared, to whom I gave my card, and we awaited his return. He soon came back, running at full speed, obsequious and smiling. The Prince was delighted to receive our visit so soon after our arrival—so at least he assured us. After this lie, he led the way, and the Prince himself received us at the door of his reception hall.

Salutations after the Chinese manner took some time, then we sat down, and I was able to observe the sovereign of Alashan. He had a very jovial face, and a smiling expression which betokened unlimited self-satisfaction.

He was disfigured by the unfortunate fact that he squinted perceptibly. By an effort of will he can, however, concentrate his gaze for a very short time like an ordinary person. For this reason, in his photographs the defect is not obvious.

He enquired the reason of our visit. I replied that I thought it necessary to inform him of the manner in which his people had disobeyed his commands. I was quite sure that he had given careful orders that we were to be taken to a

PUTTING UP THE TENT PRESENTED BY THE PRINCE OF FU-MA-FU.

[*To face p.* 98.

pleasant konkuan, but his soldiers had led us to a squalid inn where half of our baggage could not even be taken in.

Appreciating that I had given him a means of extricating himself without loss of dignity, the Prince answered that I had done well to come to him without delay, and that the men who had treated us in this way and misconstrued his clearly expressed wishes should be terribly punished. He called his major-domo, and in severe language ordered him to take us to a little palace near the town, and to see that we were supplied before evening with everything that man and beast could eat for eight days.

We were now the greatest of friends. He spoke of Pekin, of the Russians, and of the Japanese. He seemed greatly interested in the war. He could not believe that his Russian friends would admit defeat. He assured me that it was a *ruse* on their part to crush the Japanese armies when intoxicated with success. That was a regular Chinese idea! When we left him hc made us promise to return next day, when his wife, he assured us, would bc present. This was a great proof of friendship, and we could only promise to do as he wished.

The *yamen* to which we were taken was not large, but surrounded with trees, and away from noise and dust. It was composed of ten little pavilions standing apart, and would be very comfortable for some days.

The reader may judge, after this little account, of the extreme importance among these childish people of going straight to the point without hesitation, and of never allowing them to treat a European with contempt. A certain class of missionaries allow themselves and their wives to be daily insulted in the streets of the cities which they inhabit. They do this with a perpetual sickly smile upon their lips in the name of Christian charity, and this is one of the reasons why I think their existence in these parts infinitely harmful. On the other hand, it is always well in dealing with a Mandarin to leave him margin enough to let him lay the blame for his own faults upon his inferiors. He retains his dignity, and is always much more inclined to assist one.

The city of Fu-ma-fu deserves a special description. To start with, it is a remarkable fact to find in the middle of the desert a true city surrounded with walls, and encompassed by populous suburbs. The principal reason of its existence is to serve as a market between the Chinese and the Mongols—the latter being naturally robbed. The Chinese buy sheep's wool, camel's hair, horses and camels for the caravans which transport their purchase to the export centres. A good number of the Chinese buyers act for European firms at Shanghai or Tientsin, and make a profit in trading unsuspected by their employers. The Mongols buy from the Chinese flour, rice, common stuffs, coal, and ornaments, such as waist buckles, orna-

THE CENTRAL PAVILION OF THE TEMPLE OF FU-MA-FU.

[*To face p.* 100.

mented knives, necklaces of coloured glass, cotton to line clothes in winter, and, above all, shoes. For these they pay three or four times their real value.

The general appearance of the town is poor enough, the shops are little looked after, and rarely repainted, since the shopkeeper takes no pains to attract Mongol customers. Many of the houses are of mud. The palace and one or two *yamens* are grey brick. Channels of water flow across the town from east to west, and form muddy swamps here and there.

The town has not many interesting features. In the eastern portion stands a large temple in an excellent state of preservation. It is like many others in the arrangement of its buildings, but excels most of them in cleanliness, and in the care spent on the different buildings. The number of lamas is not as large as in some of the Ordos temples; but they are much more friendly.

The other object of interest is a garden 40 yards square, in which are carefully cultivated plants rare in the Alashan desert. We were made to admire more especially a fig-tree, whose miserable appearance was enough to prove that it was out of its element there. In a kind of green house, facing south, there are common plants set in pots, as one sees them in Chinese houses at Pekin.

The celebrated Prince Tuan is in retirement at Fu-ma-fu. He was living, I was told, in a *yamen* inside the town, but as I was anxious to remain in favour with the Prince of Alashan, and to obtain all the facilities I could from him, I made no detailed enquiry. Had I appeared to take too great an interest in the life and doings of his friend Tuan he would have become suspicious, and his apparent amiability and good will would have undergone a change.

While on this subject I may mention that not far from Ning-hsia the celebrated bandit, General Tong fu thiang, has set up his headquarters. It is difficult to state precisely what number of men he has under him; even the Mandarins of Ning-hsia do not know. His numbers swell according to the plenitude or emptiness of his coffers. His way of filling them is simple, and consists only in intimidating the Mandarins of all ranks, who hold charge in this part of the Province of Kansu, with the perpetual threat of letting his ruffians loose in the town.

As they are armed, or at least are supposed to be, with European rifles, of course through German contraband trade, they spread terror in all the district. According to the latest news, Tong fu thiang is ill. He is, moreover, an opium smoker, and there is a good chance that he will soon rid the world of his presence. He has the deepest hatred of Europeans, and his influence over the Mandarins may partly explain their antipathy to strangers.

To conclude, Fu-ma-fu possesses a Russian

shopkeeper, or at least a Buriat. This man, still young, acted as Mongol interpreter to one of the latest Russian explorers of the Gobi, Cassanova. Having returned to Siberia after the expedition, this gentleman, by name Badmadgaproff, decided to return to Alashan, and to settle in Fu-ma-fu as the agent of a commercial house at Urga. That at least is the story which he wished us to believe, but as a matter of fact he is settled here as political agent of Russia with the Prince of Alashan.

Being a Buriat, he speaks Mongolian and Russian; he has received some education, and at first sight would not awaken any suspicion. But if one considers the small stock in trade which he has with him, and which he does not even dispose of, one wonders what can be the commercial profit to him of his presence in this neighbourhood. The Mongols buy some coloured stuff, printed handkerchiefs, nails, and little things of this kind; but they cannot pay a high price for more valuable articles. The most they can do is to exchange the wool of their sheep for such articles, as they do with the Chinese for pairs of shoes.

The Prince himself is the only victim of the commercial aptitude of this Buriat. He pays fantastic prices for European arms and curiosities. He told me himself that he had paid 200 *taels* for an old-fashioned little Winchester carbine, which was worth twenty, and the poor man has to pay 1 *tael* for ten cartridges. He has also bought from a Chinese photographer at Tientsin an enormous photographic apparatus, with sensitive plates and chemicals enough to last for years.

He is a progressive Prince, and greatly interested in everything relating to arms and railways. He is bored to death in this corner of the desert, and has only one desire—to return to Pekin. He is not, properly speaking, Prince of Alashan, but really Prince of Kokonor. His change of kingdom is an amusing story.

Several years ago he went to Pekin to be married. The policy of the Pekin Court, to that extent wise, consists in marrying to all the Mongol kinglets princesses of the Emperor's household, thus binding them to the dynasty by the links of matrimony. The Prince of Kokonor, having married a Princess, set out again with his spouse for his distant kingdom. The Princess had no liking for this journey, and ceaselessly lamented the distance of the country in which she was to live in future. At last, having reached the opening of the Alashan desert, she absolutely refused to go a step further. The Prince in his perplexity sent couriers to Pekin to submit his case, and to beg that his spouse might be forced to be reasonable. The reply from Pekin was that if the Princess refused to go on, he must settle in the place where she had stopped, and thus the Prince of Kokonor became Prince of Alashan.

We visited him on the afternoon of the second day that we spent at Fu-ma-fu. He received

THE TEMPLE OF FU-MA-FU.

[*To face p.* 104.

us very affably, and introduced to us his wife. He has several, but this one, with whom we had the pleasure of drinking tea, is the chief wife, whom all the others must respect.

Some moments after the youngest of his sons, a boy of twenty, embellished by one of the most notable stomachs that I have ever seen on a boy of his age, dragged me into a photographic dark room arranged in European fashion, with running water for washing the plates, and different coloured lanterns. In the semi-darkness of this room I should have thought myself back in civilisation, if, on opening the door, I had not found myself confronted by a krang of polished wood, full preparations for opium smoking, a copper brasier, and carved wooden windows painted in startling colours.

We had hardly been back in our *yamen* a few minutes when some Mandarins of the Prince's following appeared, accompanied by a great number of people carrying burdens.

They came to offer us a great number of presents from their master.

To begin with, a Mongol tent of medium size, but of very thick felt, bordered with blue, and lined on the inside with green and black calico. This was a present of the greatest value for us, for I had tried in vain to secure one at any price. The idea of facing the Arctic cold of Gobi in January, with no other protection at night but the slender thickness of a canvas tent, had been depressing. This felt tent, therefore, was very welcome, and the present, moreover, would secure the respect of the Mongols wherever we went, for the Prince of Alashan had used it himself in some of his tours through his huge and yet insignificant kingdom.

After the tent came furs. Each of us received two cloaks of the finest lamb's wool, and each of our men a large and warm sheepskin.

To conclude, there were four carpets of Ning-hsia make, small, but very useful, for the inside of the tent, and, lastly, a thousand German cigarettes, very bad, which I could not make up my mind to smoke. The excellent man had really taken trouble to give us what we most needed, and had succeeded perfectly. I distributed a little money among those who had brought these presents, and told them to thank the Prince. I entrusted to them also a watch, I am afraid of no great value, which they were to give the Prince as a memento of our visit.

I finished the day by buying six fine camels for a moderate sum—40 *taels* a piece. Fu-ma-fu is the home of the biggest and finest of these animals, and I was convinced that the poor creatures which had accompanied us across the Ordos could not go much further.

On 10th October we left Fu-ma-fu at four o'clock in the afternoon. The Prince had asked me in the morning to take an observation of latitude in his presence, and I could not refuse.

The observation, followed by several cups of tea, detained us a long time, and we could only accomplish a short march of 5 miles before sunset.

We found our new tent ready pitched at the inn of Pachentsu, a Chinese house in the shade of a huge tree, and we spent an excellent night in our new dwelling.

The country to the south of Fu-ma-fu is broken by a number of small ravines, often dry, which have been dug out by the torrents from the Alashan mountains. These torrents run in parallel courses, and lose themselves in the sand at the foot of the Saï. I found no lake for them to flow into.

On the next day we went on southward. On the road which goes to Ning-hsia carts can pass along, and it is the great trade route of the country. It crosses a country of ravines and hills like those of the day before. To right and to left were some mud-built houses inhabited by Chinese and Mongols. They all more or less act as inns, and are disgustingly dirty, like all the places reserved for travelling Mongols.

We started in beautiful weather, and could distinguish the temple of Nanseshan-miao perched on the side of the Alashan mountains 14 miles to the north-east, forming a white spot against the dark rock. After the march of 15 miles, under a particularly hot sun for the time of year, we reached the inn of Turgoon.

Here the high road turns towards Ning-hsia across the mountains. As our object was to survey the west side of Alashan towards Chung-wëi, on the following day we should take a road to the south. The inn was kept by a tall Mongol woman of active appearance; her husband had been dead for some years, and she had undertaken the management of the inn in his place. With the help of her two children, boys of ten or twelve years old, she made the Chinese carters obey her with a decision and a promptitude which we admired. There was none of the Mongol timidity about her.

As the rooms in which we might have rested were in such a state of dilapidation that we could see the sky through the ceilings, we preferred to set up our comfortable felt tent in the middle of the court.

I let our animals rest for a day, for the day before they had done a march of thirteen hours without stopping, during which they had covered 30 miles to find water. We were not pressed for time, and I preferred not to tire them. They had to be fresh to face the bare desert in a few weeks' time.

On the 17th of October, leaving the ribbon of the Ning-hsia road on our left, we turned south across an undulating plain in which were many antelopes. But, owing to a vivid mirage, I was not able to bring down one of them. A hundred yards away, the plain seemed to float in the air,

THE CARAVAN ON THE MARCH IN THE DESERT OF ALASHAN.

[*To face p.* 108.

the smallest grasses looked like bushes, and it was impossible to sight a rifle. Towards evening we came amongst the mountain spurs running from east to west, which finish in the desert, growing smaller as they near the plain. Crossing picturesque gorges of rose granite and scattered boulders, we reached the well of Payen Uson, a name often given by the caravan drivers to the wells which they dig in this country. A great torrent bed ran down beside it, to lose itself in the sand.

As I have just remarked, the march of the 13th of October was a hard one. We had come out of mountain country only to cross more, and after negotiating this, having come to a plain inhabited by the Amen Uson Mongols, we had crossed a fresh chain of mountains, running in the same direction and bearing the Mongol name of Payen Sortru. Then we met with a great undulating plain with some stretches of good grass, in which antelopes abounded. This plain slopes gently down towards Chung-wëi. It is uninhabited, and seems only used for the rearing of many troops of horses, who may be seen gambolling around the stallion who orders their march, and watches over the young ones. These horses are well trained from their earliest years to the privations and hardships of desert life. They cover enormous distances at a canter, when thirst forces them to come to the wells to drink. In winter they drink the snow, and scratch the surface hardened by the frost to reach the dry grass under it.

At the wells of Oiero Ottock, which we reached at ten o'clock at night, we found some Chinese merchants installed. Installed is perhaps euphuistic, for they were smoking their opium between two stuff hangings with a camel's saddle for a roof. They were carrying loads of coarse stuffs and of opium to Fu-ma-fu. The next day at six o'clock they started with the first rays of the sun, and towards noon, when we were lazily resting, we saw a line of Chinese carts approaching, drawn by mules and driven by inhabitants of Chung-wëi, who were carrying forage for the winter to support some of the Prince's animals. This was the first time that I had seen Mongols take such precautions for their beasts.

At the end of the day I heard the voices of my men rising in a discussion which seemed likely to become serious. I went to the spot at once, and enquired into the facts which were causing so much indignation on the part of my caravan men. I learnt that Norbo, when about to mend the saddle of one of the camels under his care, had found the straw out of two saddles removed. In the course of his enquiries he became convinced that the carters had stolen the straw to give it to their mules, which were eating it at that moment. Upon this evidence, the carters having nothing to urge in defence, I ordered twice the value of the straw to be taken from their carts, and told them to leave at once, though the next well was a good distance off. I had no desire to let these marauders spend the night near our baggage, having no confidence in the watch kept by my people.

The next day's journey was not marked by any accident. We started early, and having crossed the bed of a river which exists only in the rainy season, the bottom of which was covered with a blood red plant, we covered a small stage, and encamped at the well of Ulan Utbuc. Here again we met other caravans. The road to Fu-ma-fu seemed well frequented. The high hills had disappeared, and instead of them were deep hollows and sandy plateaus. Near the well the æolian erosion had made terraces of red clay in strange shapes.

The next day we reached Chung-wëi, after a march of about 14 miles. As we drew near this town, the sand collected in great quantities till it formed large sand-hills, marked at the foot by the tracks of antelopes.

We passed the Obo of Sare, the border mark between Mongolia and China, and soon after crossed the great wall, here a little mound hardly worth noticing.

Crossing the ridges and valleys of sand which kept increasing in size, we came down towards Chung-wëi, and suddenly saw before us the wide plain in the middle of which this town is built, not far from the Yellow River.

During the flood of the preceding months, the whole plain had been under water, and in many places large swamps still remained. When we had left the wall of sand and begun to cross the field I observed that these swamps were covered with ducks, geese, and wild swans, in great abundance. They are easily killed, since, except the swans, they are scarcely wild, as the Chinese do not shoot these birds. A few shots obtained for us an abundance of succulent food, that would enable us to dispense for some time with the mutton of which we were so tired.

The house which the Mandarins had prepared for us was that of a Chinese merchant, the agent of a firm in Shanghai for the purchase of wool. Three small rooms, clean and warm enough, were put at our disposal, whilst the men and animals were comfortably housed in large rooms with mud walls, and in fine stables.

Seeing that we should be comfortable there for a stay of some days I decided to send Norbo back to Fu-ma-fu to buy twenty other camels. The information that I had received proved beyond doubt that the price of one of these animals at Lian-chou or at Liang-chou would be much higher than that which I had had to pay at Fu-ma-fu; and I had every advantage to gain in buying all my animals in that town, seeing that not only was their price less, but that they were stronger and not injured by badly weighted loads, as those that I could obtain on the other side of the Great Wall were likely to be.

The town of Chung-wëi is not large. Within its walls many dwellings are in ruins and, beyond the wool trade, which is important, there is not much traffic. Several European firms keep agents there to buy wool. On the road to Ning-hsia, following the river front, was formerly a bastion three-quarters of a mile from that town. Around its ruins, has grown up the suburb in which we were temporary residents.

The situation of the city is peculiar. High ridges of sand surround it on the north and west, at varying distances never more than 7 miles away, which I have noticed before. The lines of these ridges all run from east to west, and as far as I could ascertain, the wind blows steadily in this direction during almost the whole year. On the south of the city flows the mighty Yellow River, to the east stretches the plain, through which the river has cut its channel. There is only one high road, that from Ning-hsia to Liang-chou. I do not reckon amongst high roads that by which we had come from Fu-ma-fu.

The alluvial plain which surrounds the city is remarkably fertile. But at times the harvest is lost, owing to too sudden a rising of the river, whose waters destroy everything within their reach.

We spent some time in this little Chinese town in the greatest peace. The Mandarins visited us, and I returned their civility. One day, when we had invited them to a great feast, one of them begged me to allow him to retire into the bedroom to smoke opium. He assured me that he could not spend an hour without smoking. I asked him to retire to his own *yamen* since we particularly disliked the smell of opium. We have never seen him since, and are not sorry. It will hardly be believed that he was not more than twenty-two years old.

Our greatest pleasure was to shoot in the neighbourhood of the town, where a great variety of game was to be found. This was our bag for five days: thirty ducks, three geese, and a wild swan. The flesh of the swan is uneatable, but its magnificent white down makes a very soft cushion. In connection with shooting I recollect a funny story. The military Mandarin in command at Chung-wëi (he commanded perhaps fifty men), had a request conveyed to me that he might shoot with me. Naturally I agreed to his wish and took him with us. It took me a quarter of an hour to drive into his sluggish brain the chief precautions that he must take to avoid accidents, and we began shooting.

He let off his first shot too soon and landed a charge of small shot in the foot of one of the soldiers in attendance. Luckily the range was a long one, and the man was not seriously hurt. His second and third shot were attended neither by success nor by disaster. Just as he was going to fire his fourth, he unfortunately slipped at the side of a ditch and took a mud bath. That was enough for him. Climbing upon his mule, he ambled off at full speed towards his *yamen*, without thinking of bidding us good-bye.

I took also during these fifteen days a series of meteorological observations which may be useful, as making known the pressures which prevail in autumn in this part of the world.

On the 24th of October there was a heavy fall of snow, and the courtyard of our dwelling, as well as all the streets and valleys, became a dirty drain. All active life was suspended, and our existence became indescribably monotonous. I think that we should have gone mad with boredom if we had had to live long shut up in a Chinese town. During the bad season of the rains there is nothing whatever to do. Social life exists but little in China. Friends rarely visit one another, there are no places of public entertainment except the sacred theatre where plays are given only on certain occasions, and which is far from amusing even for the Chinese. After some fearfully unoccupied days, I began to understand the huge influence over this nation of the opium which produces a feeling of lassitude and of forgetfulness of the idea of time. There is practically no communication with the rest of the world. News spreads from the leading city of the province to the small towns by means of carters and caravan drivers, but after having passed through so many mouths it is no longer recognisable, and is wholly devoid of interest.

The cities which have telegraphic and postal communications are certainly better off, but even here the mistakes, the delays, and the lies in which these departments excel in China have to be reckoned with. Considering that a letter written at Liang-chou and addressed to Europe cannot receive an answer before seven or eight months, it is not too much to state that life is not worth living in the interior of China, except for some devoted missionaries and others, who have some special vocation there.

On the 26th I received a visit from a merchant of the town, who came to ask me whether I should not like to go and see the silver mines close to Ping-liang-fu, about 100 miles to the south-east, which he said were wonderful. His plan was extremely simple. After inspecting the mines, I was to get leave to work them from the Governor of Kansu, and I was then to pay my friend a large percentage on the profit, in return for his zeal in putting me on to such a good thing. There was only one slight objection, merely that the Governor has never made any concessions to Europeans except on excellent terms for himself, and that the agents of the King of Belgium at Liang-chou have obtained nothing from him in spite of all their efforts. So I sent the merchant about his business and patiently awaited Norbo's return.

He arrived from Fu-ma-fu with twenty camels, which were far from satisfying my desires. Most of them were thin and weak. To get a better idea of their condition I had the saddles removed from their backs, and discovered that two of the animals were badly galled. Norbo seemed even more astonished than I. He had bought the camels with the saddles on, and never for a moment suspected that his Mongol brothers would play him such a dirty trick. He had paid a very high price for them, and this trusty servant must have made a handsome profit on the account which he presented to me. I could do nothing but set out with these sorry animals, and do my best to feed them up well before using them in January in the Gobi.

Without wasting time we left Chung-wëi by noon; the camels which had arrived the day before were loaded, and the long procession filed down the street, the bells which the leaders carried on their necks giving notice of their approach.

During the first stage we travelled towards the south-west on the stones of an old bed of the Yellow River, which covered, in the dawn of history, an enormous extent of ground. Compared with what it has been, this huge river seems to-day a feeble stream. Its current is fairly swift, and it works the wheels of two tanneries which have been erected on its bank. Further along, in front of the village of Yula, there is a rapid, which makes its presence known from afar by the flashing of its water. To avoid this danger, and to allow the boats that go down the river to make a safe passage, a small canal, large enough for three boats abreast, has been cleverly constructed, which runs alongside of the river, and enters it again when the current has calmed down.

On this night one of the best horses was attacked by fever. The poor beast shivered like an aspen, and seemed to me very ill; but the men, having held a consultation, went up to the animal, and one of them burnt a roll of thick paper under its nostrils while the others held it still. They assured me that after this treatment, or rather torture, the beast would soon recover its normal condition, and in fact two hours later it ate its corn greedily.

At this point the road left the river, to cross ridges of sand very lofty and difficult to climb because of the extreme dryness of the sand which gave way under the feet. The river itself issues from a narrow gorge, and it is impossible to follow its course up to Liang-chou. The mountains finish abruptly at more points than one, and forbid a passage along the bed, and the Chinese have not thought it necessary to undertake the hard work which a road in those places would involve. The sand, therefore, must be crossed, and one must travel towards the south-west for a long distance before turning back in a south-easterly direction towards Liang-chou. Carts, of course, cannot overcome the great obstacle caused by the sand-hills. They have to cross the river, travel for some distance on the right bank, and recross the river after having passed the ridges of sand. A caravan with camels and horses can avoid these transhipments, but has to climb a steep ascent, and put in a tiring stage on shifting ground.

In spite of all our efforts, and even some rude speeches, I had not been able at Chung-wëi to escape the inevitable and hateful escort of a little fat Mandarin and five thieving soldiers. After one day's march they began to get on our nerves. They tried to persuade my men to share with them the provisions which I had bought for the journey. I intervened in time to stop this little game; but one of the soldiers then declared that he would go no further with me if he was not fed. To my mind that was an additional reason for refusing. The following morning he had deserted.

No doubt he would plunder in the neighbourhood until his companions returned from Liang-chou, and would lay all the thefts which he committed at the door of the "foreign devils." On various occasions I had asked the Mandarin in command in the towns where our escorts were appointed whether I had to furnish their ordinary food, flour and rice, to the soldiers. I always received the same answer, that I had not to think of anything, and that they had to provide for their own nourishment. It is certainly a fact, none the less, that these men receive no provision when they leave their home to accompany a traveller. The Mandarin knows it, and in this way makes himself an accessory to their brigandage. The result is that, when robbed, the peasants dare not bring complaints, since they know that their judge is himself the chief culprit of whom they will have to complain.

From Chung-wëi we had risen more than 1,800 feet, and at this season of the year this slight change in latitude caused a much greater change in the temperature. It was very cold at night, and the thermometer hardly rose above freezing point by day, whenever the sun retired for a few moments behind a veil of clouds.

We were on a great plateau whose northern side sloped gently down to Alashan, and whose southern flank was supported by a low chain of mountains. From the village of Siwantnatse, at which we had halted, and which is only a miserable hamlet, we saw in the clear splendour of day the chain of the Alashan mountains defined against the north-east, and standing out from the plain, strongly coloured in dark blue and mauve. In the earlier part of the day the road had followed the course of a tributary of the Yellow River, and all along it we had come across ancient beacon towers, of which the authorities made use in old times to communicate interesting events quickly from one point to another. Torches in varying numbers served as an alphabet.

On the 4th of November, the camel drivers asked me to give the animals a little rest. Those that they had recently bought were not yet in training for daily marches. I hesitated a little, for I thought that this proposal was due to laziness rather than to their concern about the camels; but having inspected the animals I decided to halt for one day at the village of Yang pri choui — composed of six houses. Instead of devouring with eagerness the grass which was fairly good many of the camels crouched on the ground, their long necks extended and their eyes closed, which is always a sign of fatigue. I wondered anxiously what use I could make of them, unless I got them into better condition, in a country where long halts are not possible.

The day was not entirely wasted. I took some observations with an eclimeter to determine the height of some snow peaks far to the west.

Towards evening, one of the men, Sarol, brought to us four lamas, whose miserable appearance and unwontedly humble attitude showed that something important had happened.

The poor wretches had come from Pekin, and were going on pilgrimage to Kumbum. They had quitted the capital of the celestial Empire six months before, and had gone first to Utaïshan, had then continued their journey by the Shansi, up to Ning-hsia, and had been delayed at Yang pri choui for several months, as the result of a night attack.

On their arrival, they had pitched their tent at a short distance from the village, where, incidentally, was a garrison of ten soldiers, posted for the suppression of brigands, thinking themselves perfectly safe under the protection of the authorities. But in the middle of the night they were suddenly and treacherously attacked by some gentlemen armed with swords and Mongol rifles, who stole the money which the pilgrims were taking to Kumbum as an offering from their monastery, and left them in the most pitiable condition.

One of them had his neck nearly severed, another had lost an ear and was pierced in the shoulder, a third had his elbow cut open by a sword stroke, and the fourth, in defending himself had seized in his hands the sword of his assailant, and had thus received a most painful wound.

Since then they had remained where we found them, at first too much damaged to travel, and, when they had partly recovered, too much afraid. Furthermore, they had not been allowed to join any large caravan travelling in comparative safety, and they had come to beg us to allow them to travel with us on the next day. They were certain that the brigands would never attack a company, however small, commanded by a European, and armed with repeating rifles.

We granted their request through sheer humanity; but we gave the men strict orders to keep a keen eye upon their behaviour and movements, for your lama is the most hypocritical, insinuating, and skilful of thieves.

Our new travelling companions appeared punctually at the hour of our departure, in the most grotesque dress. The weakest of them, with the wounded neck, was seated on an unfortunate little donkey, a tiny animal which could hardly manage to put one foot before the other. The three stronger lamas walked, very gloomy, and pushing before them two little asses on which they had put the little that remained to them, a small tent in rags, some sheepskins on which they slept, and some 10 lbs. of flour.

The only interest attaching to our journey on that day was that we turned south, and left the plateau which commands the desert of Alashan. We entered a little winding valley, and at once the temperature seemed to rise, and the wind was less cutting. After having descended for 16 miles a series of hollows, we reached the little town of Sutran. According to custom, the Mandarin sent one of his followers to present his card to us, and to greet us in his name. This man brought us to a fairly clean little house, and invited us to take possession of it, when, suddenly, just as I was ordering the camels to be unloaded, the Mandarin himself arrived, one of the most curious specimens of his kind that I have ever met.

Advancing towards us with extended arms, he performed several salutations. Then, suddenly, he rushed towards me and pressed me to his chest, with every sign of the keenest emotion. My resistance was useless, he repeated this comedy, and on its conclusion begged us to follow him to his *yamen*, where he had prepared a room for us.

The *yamen* was one of the poorest, made of mud, painted white, and ornamented here and there with large rings of red. The whole building was shaky, and suited the wretched little town in the midst of which it was built.

But the reception prepared for us was as careful as could be. We were given Chinese brandy instead of tea, and our host drank a full cup of it. I began to understand the strangeness of his behaviour. He was a drunkard, and seemed to have prepared for our reception by the most copious libations. I afterwards learned from his servants that their master was never sober to their knowledge, and that no man from there to Liang-chou could drink so much brandy without falling flat on the floor.

I decided to spend a day at Sutran with the object of making a map of the surrounding mountains. The Mandarin could not express his joy at this news, and finally drunk off at a gulp another cup of his favourite beverage.

The reader may be interested to know the pecuniary resources and the occupations of these small Mandarins. An officer of the blue button, like the one at Sutran, receives a fixed salary of 400 *taels*—about £48 a year. When I say that he receives this pay, I mean that he is supposed to, but for a number of reasons which would take too long to explain, and which are more or less due to the rapacity of his immediate superiors, he seldom handles it. On his side he has to support a certain number of soldiers, subordinates of all kinds, a steward, some beggars, himself, and his family.

In China living is evidently cheap; but it is impossible to live on nothing, even on the edge of the Alashan desert. What, then, can our Mandarin do, since he gets little or no money? He must oppress the people until he obtains his requirements, and more besides. He has, in fact, paid a certain price for his post, and he naturally desires to recover his expenses. Furthermore, if he wishes to get on, and have a brilliant career, he must save a sufficient sum during his three years' occupation to buy a higher post, which will probably cost him double what he paid for that in which he is at the moment exercising a semblance of authority. He must sell justice, make a profit out of criminals, force lawsuits upon rich merchants, allow his soldiers to rob, and omit to pay his debts. In this way the Chinese Mandarins, from the highest to the lowest, are rotten to the core, and to change this deplorable state of things, which is at the bottom of Chinese stagnation, prodigious efforts are needed, and a lapse of time of which those who speak of the regeneration of this huge empire have no conception.

All the forces, for good and evil, in this populous country are not centred round Canton, Hong Kong, Shanghai, Tientsin, and Pekin, or in the neighbourhood of the open ports, and only a very small fraction of the people has been impressed and affected by the presence of the Europeans with whom they are in frequent and compulsory contact. Ninety per cent. of the Chinese people have not the least idea of our ways and our ideas, and we shall have to overcome the formidable resistance of all the authorities who are profiting by the actual state of things before we can arrive at any practical result. In that day we shall perhaps bitterly regret that we did not leave the terrible monster who will then rise before us, crouching in his muddy lair.

The soldiers, who keep guard at the *yamen* act as police, receive pay ranging from 2 to 3 *taels* a month. They all smoke opium, and their pay is just enough to enable them to indulge in this vice. On what then do their families subsist? On thefts protected and unpunished, and, above all, on blackmail. That is the chief means of extracting money from the tradesman. Give me so much or I will denounce you to the Mandarin. The wretched trader pays, and unless he leaves the city and appears in his new home as a poor man, he will die a beggar. An old comic opera assures us: *La Chine est un pays charmant.*

On leaving Sutran, we passed a great number of towns, villages, and fortified farms. The last Mussulmans rebellion which caused fearful ravages all through Kansu caused the elevation here and there of fortified dwellings surrounded by great mud walls, sometimes more than 20 feet high, with one or two towers which command the country, and act as bastions. Inside these walls is a path on which are heaped broken stones and large pebbles. Very rarely the inhabitants possess a bad rifle or a jagged sword. Their one hope and resource lies in their implements of work, and in these heaps of stones. Sometimes above the entrance gate is a turret built out like a balcony. Through a hole in the flooring of this the defenders, in case of attacks, would try to throw upon their assailants boiling water, bricks, and anything that might wound or kill.

Before the Mussulmans spread on all sides with fire and sword, these farms, which look so warlike to-day, were only surrounded by walls of moderate height. The difference in colour between the upper and lower portions shows that they have only been recently fortified.

What caused, and probably would again cause the ruin of these unlucky peasants if a new rebellion broke out, is their want of united action.

Each farmer took refuge in his own farm, with his wives, children, and servants, in all perhaps ten or fifteen persons of both sexes, and tried to beat off the enemy in his own way. These isolated dwellings were taken and burnt one after another. The conquering assailants murdered and plundered, though they were not numerous, and had only imperfect weapons like those of their victims.

The general aspect of the country is consequently most picturesque, and we felt as if we were travelling in the Middle Ages in the days of bandits and highwaymen, of strong castles and civil wars.

Before concluding our march for the night, and halting at the little fortified village of Sacretien we crossed a ridge about 1,200 feet high, around which lay numerous deposits of coal, scattered on the surface of the ground. The inhabitants of the country profit by these abundant riches, and use them for immediate needs. Their methods of work are very primitive. Wherever the precious mineral protrudes above the surface, they attack it with pickaxes, and dig a hole never more than 10 yards deep. Whether the vein is exhausted or not, they abandon it, for fear the earth should fall in. They will not take the trouble to prop up the walls of the cavity which they have made. They rarely follow the vein to its full extent. That would compel skilled work, which they consider useless and costly, while a little further on they

A ROAD IN KANSU.

[To face p. 128.

can tap fresh supplies of coal on the ground level without trouble or expense.

Kansu is extremely rich in mines of all sorts —coal, silver, gold, tin, zinc, copper, and iron. Unfortunately communications between this remote province and the rest of the world are costly and lengthy, and certain minerals, such as coal, which would yield large profits under other conditions, must remain unproductive until the conditions for working them improve.

The coal of these mines is burnt in all this district as far as Liang-chou. Near this capital are other very rich mines.

We continued a monotonous journey in a country full of farms, destroyed by Mussulmans, and small fortifications of the kind that I have already described.

In the morning a disagreeable surprise awaited us. Three of the camels, and three of the best, were absolutely incapable of starting. They seemed drunk, with their legs straddling to keep their balance, their heads hanging, their eyes closed, their thick lips slobbering. Every effort to make them advance or move being vain, I was obliged to wait for another day, for I could not lose these three animals. As for leaving them behind, and committing them to the care of the peasants, they might just as well have been sacrificed at once.

The camels had been poisoned by a plant with a thin stem and a red corolla, which grew in the neighbourhood. Oddly enough, the horses, mules, and asses had eaten this plant with impunity. Only the camels had suffered from it.

The men began at once a course of treatment which consisted in beating the animals with sticks until they tried to move. As a result, they fell heavily to the ground, and lay with their necks stretched out in front. Then the men opened the animal's mouths and poured into them a draught difficult to specify, but in which ammonia played a great part. Then they let the sick beasts rest near the tents, while the others were peacefully feeding in a part of the plain where the dreadful plant did not seem to have taken root.

Towards evening, the Mongol Norbo asked me for some *sapeques* to buy aniseed with from a neighbouring farm. He crushed it, mixed it with flour, and made pills of it, which he caused the camels to swallow. A little while after two of them were strong enough to get up and take a few steps. If not loaded, they would be able to manage the march of the next day. I was not so happy about the third, which had not opened its eyes all day, and which was dropping a great deal of foul smelling saliva from its mouth.

That night was a disturbed one. At about eleven o'clock I suddenly heard a noise of hoofs and of frightened neighing. Seizing a carbine, which I always kept loaded, I ran out, and for some time could distinguish nothing in the dense darkness of the night; I heard the men calling to one another, and I went towards them. "A wolf had carried off the chronometer mule," they told me, shivering with fright. I handed rifles to two of them, and we started in pursuit, but only met with a few casual falls, due to the invisible inequalities of the ground.

In the morning I examined the tracks left by our nocturnal assailant. I could easily see from the size of the pads and the length of the claws that it was no wolf, but a panther, that had carried one of our beasts off. I questioned some countrymen who had been drawn to the spot by the news of the incident, and they assured me that sometimes panthers of great size come down to the plain in search of food, and carry off their sheep.

The half-eaten carcass of the mule lay a few hundred paces away.

On 13th November the cold was intense. Snow was falling fast, and under these conditions our march was a trying one. The men were grumbling; they always wanted to stop as soon as the temperature became unpleasant. Their sighs and sulky faces furnished us with our only entertainment on this hateful day. We slept in a tiny house, which we hunted out in the middle of a small town strikingly like a mediæval stronghold, with its moats, dungeons, and fortified gateway. Its three hundred inhabitants were huddled inside it, terrified at the sight of us.

In the night the temperature went down to 10°, and the snow was frozen hard. Luckily, we should reach Liang-chou on the next day.

CHAPTER V

THROUGH KANSU

THE city of Liang-chou, the capital of the Province of Kansu, is very picturesquely situated. Hemmed in on one side by the Yellow River it extends over a large plain between three valleys, and contains a population reckoned at a million souls. I think this number greatly exaggerated. I should consider the half of it a correct estimate. The most curious feature of Liang-chou is the bridge of boats which joins the two banks of the Hoang Ho. This bridge is made up of a large number of boats on which has been set a kind of pontoon, constructed of roughly joined planks of wood, so that there is a certain amount of danger in crossing it. The boats are bound together by huge iron chains running from end to end of the bridge. If the iron employed were of better quality a band of half the diameter would suffice. The current is not very rapid, and the danger of a breach is confined to the time of the melting of the snows, when large blocks of ice are carried down by the water. The city inserts a large sum in its budget every year for the upkeep of the bridge; but, owing to the usual system of plunder, very little of it is spent in that way.

Below the bridge some strange rafts may be seen on the muddy water, made of inflated sheep-skins tied together with ropes. A deck thrown over these bladders is more or less firmly attached, and we have before us the kind of vessel which transports travellers and trade from Liang-chou to Ning-hsia. An ordinary wooden boat would not be able to resist the rapids, which pass, as I have noted before, between pointed rocks standing close together, and swing round sometimes actually at right angles. Even these boats are not safe, and five years ago an unfortunate European met his death under sad circumstances not far from Liang-chou. In endeavouring to escape from a threatened massacre, he took refuge on one of these rafts, and entrusted himself to some inexperienced boatmen who, at the first rapid, were unable to control the craft. It perished, with all on board, in the waters.

The barracks, parade ground, and rifle range of the Liang-chou garrison are not far away, opposite the eastern gate. I was not able to ascertain how many men the garrison was supposed to consist of, but certainly the Governor does all in his power to improve his soldiers. The men are far inferior none the less to those whom we reviewed at Kwei-hua-cheng. I witnessed some of their drills, and can state that they have still much to learn before they will even be presentable.

Liang-chou possesses also a factory of arms, existing in a large and clean building, originally built by a German company which attempted to manufacture cloth. Had the company succeeded its profits would have been enormous; but it had to fight complete corruption and sordid greed, and was obliged to close its doors in total failure.

The factory of arms produces rifles such as our grandfathers used a century ago. They are hammer guns well enough made for arms of this kind, but quite incapable of resisting the smallest troop in modern warfare. A great number of these rifles are delivered at Sining-fu, where they are bought at a high price by Tibetan caravan drivers, who always dread the attacks of robbers between Sining-fu and Lhasa. At Liang-chou the price of one of these weapons is 9 *taels*.

It is also possible at Liang-chou to procure arms made in and imported from Germany, Mausers, and Mannlichers, with their cartridges. Every one knows, but nobody mentions, the source whence they come, and the illicit contraband of which the importers are guilty.

While at Liang-chou we received the kindest hospitality from Mr Splingaert, originally a Belgian, now a naturalised Chinaman. He is one of the only Europeans I believe who has held for a long time an administrative post in the interior of China. He is a Mandarin of the red button, both civil and military, and has received the celebrated decoration of the ten thousand families.

That decoration is as follows: When a Mandarin, in charge of a great city, has satisfied the inhabitants by his honesty and good administration, a certain number of families, ten thousand, join in offering him three large parasols, to which are attached a number of small black and yellow silk streamers, one for each family, and inscribed with its name. They also present to him a dress of black and yellow silk with inscriptions. The Mandarin has the right to wear this dress at an audience of the Emperor, and thus prove to his master his qualities as a servant and officer.

Another and much commoner mark of the esteem in which an officer is held is the hanging up in a small cage of wood at the entrance to the town, under the arch of the chief gate, of a pair of his shoes when he leaves the town. All who have visited Chinese cities must have noticed these cages.

At Liang-chou we met two German explorers, Lieutenant Filchner and Doctor Taffel. The lieutenant had come from Shanghai to Liang-chou by the well-known high road, accompanied by his wife; but the lady had stayed at Sining-fu with the representatives of the China Inland Mission, dreading the weary journey through Tibet, while the two explorers were doing their best to reach the Oring Nor.

They had thought it advisable to have recourse to the Chinese forces to assist them on their journey, and had appealed to the military Mandarin of Sining-fu. He had given them a strong escort of well-armed soldiers, and one of his own official tents, with a view to impressing the inhabitants of that undoubtedly dangerous portion of Tibet.

But all these precautions proved useless, for they were attacked by a troop of armed Tibetans, who began to fire on them at night after they had come out of a defile. The European caravan suffered no loss; but the next morning they judged it prudent to retreat at full speed, leaving their baggage behind. They reached Yunnan, and thence Liang-chou and Sining-fu.

The result of their expedition strengthened the resolution which we had long formed to rely solely on our own force in crossing Tibet, and to avoid everything which might suggest to the Tibetans that we had any connection with the Chinese authorities. Their hatred and contempt for the Chinese is so strong that that feeling alone will drive them to attack a convoy which they would probably allow to pass unmolested without an armed escort. The presence of an escort shows them that the explorers are afraid of them, which incites them to brigandage. This theory was justified by experience.

Liang-chou is also the principal site of the mining agents of King Leopold, who have been vainly trying to acquire mining concessions for years, with more perseverance than knowledge of the situation.

Strangers seem to be absolutely loathed at Liang-chou. It is no rare experience to be insulted in the open street by persons of all classes, and to have the harmless but exasperating salutation of "foreign devil" dinned into one's ears. The Mandarins are difficult of approach, for they follow the example of their chief, the Governor, who considers all Europeans to be dust under his feet, and treats them with the most perfect unconcern. In spite of treaties, in his official relations with the missionary bishops, he never gives them the titles conferred upon them by the convention signed by Mr Gerard. I do not think that the convention is to be approved of, since it degrades Europeans by definitely placing most of them lower than some Chinese officials in its endeavour to raise the prestige of missionaries—but anything once signed should be held to.

On one of the walls of the city pamphlets were stuck up, vilifying and cursing Europeans. Shortly before our arrival, abuse of Mr Splingaert had been written up, Chinese Mandarin of high rank as he was. There is no open declaration of war, but the latent hatred is only waiting the signal to break out.

It is practically useless to appeal to Chinese tribunals for justice to secure the condemnation of the insolent ruffians who try to make Europeans a popular laughing-stock in broad daylight in the open street.

While we were there, a Boxer publicly conducted so active a propaganda that the magistrates could not shut their eyes to it. They arrested the gentleman and sentenced him to a very small number of strokes with a bamboo, and left him free to begin again. Within six months of the troubles of 1900 this man would have been beheaded. Such is the change already!

While waiting at Liang-chou I did my best to improve the condition of my caravan camels. Many were hurt, and all very thin. As I was constantly told that our caravan drivers were neither experienced nor clever enough to keep them healthy, I sent for a camel driver named Lao Yang from Liang-chou. He had a great reputation for his skill, and had served under Mr Splingaert on one of his many journeys, when he acted as secretary to Baron von Reichtoffen on his celebrated expedition.

When Lao Yang had arrived and taken command of our little troop we had no more reason to delay at Liang-chou, and, in spite of the kind hospitality offered us, we decided to start again.

Our course, before entering the Gobi Desert, included a diversion to Sining-fu and Kumbum.

I shall not enter upon a detailed account of this road, not specially interesting, since it has been travelled over by all the explorers and missionaries who have gone to Kansu.

The road leaves the river and leads to Ping-fan, a sub-prefectoral town, which commands the high road to Liang-chou and Sining-fu. It follows the windings of a little tributary of the Yellow River, down hill all the way, across lofty and picturesque terraces of red clay which seem to keep to an altitude of 4,000 or 5,000 feet, without exceeding it. The population, without being numerous, seems prosperous enough, and food and lodging are easily found by the traveller.

Having reached Ping-fan on the 3rd of December we decided to send all the camels and two-thirds of the men to wait for us at Liang-chou, not thinking it worth while to take them round by Sining-fu. The renowned Lao Yang assured us with much gesticulation that he knew of an excellent place not far away, and to the west of Liang-chou, where the animals would find plenty of food, and would visibly improve their condition in three weeks.

We only kept with us what we wanted and a little money. We hired two carriages, or rather two springless carts, covered with a straw roof, in which to journey to Sining-fu. Each cart cost 20 *taels* and was drawn by a horse and a mule in tandem—strong animals both. I promised the drivers a little extra pay if they covered the 340 *lis* (115 miles) between Ping-fan and Sining-fu in four days. This distance could easily be covered, were it not for the intervention of steep ups and downs, and the crossing of a ferry.

We settled ourselves as comfortably as possible amongst bundles in one of the carts, and having put all our men into the other, started off at a

FIRST SNOWS, NEAR LIANG-TCHOU-FU.

[*To face p.* 140.

good pace, while our caravan of camels moved slowly northward under the noisy and tumultuous orders of Lao Yang.

We arrived at the day and hour fixed; but we had some trouble in doing it. After the first 30 miles, the fine rapture of the drivers and their animals began to fail; after 60 miles, the carts crawled. We contrived it by making night marches, sleeping in the carts.

Sining-fu is a very picturesque city, not only owing to its position, but chiefly because of the number of different races which contribute to its population.

In the chief streets, lined by shops of all kinds, may be seen Chinese from all parts of China, Tibetans from the North and from Lhasa, Ordos Mongols and Mongols from Tsaidam, Kansu Mussulmans and Mussulmans from Kashgar; aboriginals, whose ancient history can hardly be traced, and half Russianised Buriats—occasionally even a Hindu. *Pêle mêle,* crowded together, the naked shoulder of a Tibetan against the blue cloth of the Chinaman, they discuss for an interminable time the price of a box of European matches or of a small looking-glass. The pointed coiffure of the bold-looking Tibetan women overtops the mass of dirty caps with red silk buttons worn by the Chinese. All are busy and interested, for Sining-fu is the chief emporium of civilisation for a large portion of the world. Here the great caravans that come twice in the year from Lhasa and Shigatse obtain what they require. Through Sining-fu, the news of China reaches the centre of the desert, and along with the cheap articles which the common Tibetans can afford to buy. Whether all these races are always on the best of terms with one another it would be hard to say; but there did not seem to be an unusual amount of quarrels and discussions. All visitors to Sining-fu seem chiefly animated by the desire to satisfy their curiosity, to amuse themselves, and to buy as much as possible at small expense.

The Rev. Mr Ridley, of the China Inland Mission, kindly came to see us, and gave us interesting details about the country which he knows through and through. I am indebted to him for a chart of the distribution of the different nations in the neighbourhood of Sining-fu, which is full of interest.

As we did not intend to make a long stay at Sining-fu, we decided to go the next day to the famous monastery of Kumbum, so much extolled and celebrated by the various travellers who have seen it, from the Fathers Huc and Gabet, down to the most recent explorers, for example, Sven Hedin.

This monastery was the principal cause of our visit to this portion of Kansu.

We could not start before midday. We had to hire some horses, and as those which had been brought to us in the morning were unfit for use, we had to wait several hours before we could obtain suitable animals.

There was nothing remarkable about the first portion of the road, which followed the bed of the river until it turned at right angles to follow the course of a small tributary, near the source of which stands the great monastery. We advanced at a good pace, not being burdened with a numerous following or much luggage. We only had with us a few soldiers, and an officer of low rank whom the Mandarin in charge of the Tibetans had thrust upon us, under the pretext that we should be better treated by the lamas.

One of our own men amused us greatly by the exuberant joy which he exhibited without ceasing all the way. He was Sarol, the Mongol. He had put on his finest clothes to go to Kumbum, and, even then, not considering himself sufficiently sumptuously attired, had borrowed various ornaments on all sides. It was a great day for that good Mongol, the fact of having gone to Kumbum more or less as a pilgrim gave him an absolute right to everlasting happiness, and meanwhile undoubtedly caused him great terrestrial pleasure. He gesticulated, shouted, yelled, sang out of tune, and galloped about, trying to make his pony perform skilful evolutions on the edge of the ditches, until both pony and rider eventually rolled over on a stretch of thick mud.

Having passed several mills, worked by the swift current of the little river, we came in sight of Kumbum. But night was now beginning to fall, and we had to continue our way by the light of the many lamps which shone out on all sides from the different buildings of the temple, with the most pleasing and picturesque effect.

Some lamas, warned of our arrival, were waiting for us near a dimly lighted porch leading to a large inner court. They led us politely to the little room which had been reserved for us, which we reached by climbing an unsteady ladder serving for a staircase.

We found a meal, consisting of butter, tea, and some cakes, cooked in the Chinese manner, laid in a room some 15 or 18 feet square, with a wooden floor, ceiling, and wainscoting. After bidding us good-night, the lamas retired, fingering the small beads of their rosaries. We woke in the night nearly suffocated, and having lit a candle we found a thick and bitter cloud of smoke coming into our room through the cracks in the flooring. Some pilgrims had made a fire in the room under ours, and were peacefully cooking their dinner with no idea that they were smoking us out. After a short parley, they laughingly consented to remove their kitchen and their fire to the middle of the court. At dawn some lamas came and knocked at the door, and presented us with a piece of silk from the Grand Lama. They were to be our guides over the monastery.

The court of the house in which we had spent the night presented an attractive spectacle. A large number of Tibetans, men, women, and children, were warming themselves in the sun, or finishing their meals, and as the sun gradually warmed the air, partly threw off their sheepskin clothes, exposing their naked and sinewy shoulders. All were wearing the little pointed cap, which gives so unwarlike a look to Tibetan soldiers, but is not without originality.

We then began our inspection of the different temples. All are well kept up, and some of them richly ornamented. On some pillars of the largest hall panther and leopard skins were hung—very old, and covered with dust. Others were covered with very well-worked Turkistan carpets. There were statues like those in other temples, but more richly decorated, and, as elsewhere, pictures representing scenes in Buddha's life. The true wealth of Kumbum lies in its precious collection of Buddhist sacred books, which are of the highest interest to scholars of this difficult and arduous science, such as Rockhill, but which leave the ordinary traveller unmoved. These books are usually made up of separate pamphlets pressed together between two pieces of painted carved wood, and bound together by rolls of embroidery.

One specially interesting spot is where all the pilgrims prostrate themselves at full length in homage to the divine Buddha. In front of the open gates of a small temple some planks are laid on the ground, which are longer and broader than the length and breadth of a man. The pilgrims prostrate themselves on these boards, sliding forward on the palms of their hands until their whole body is resting on the ground. Then they rest, and prostrate themselves again, until they are turned out by the attendants. Some lamas keep order and receive the offerings.

We were surrounded by a group of inquisitive lamas. They were also very evil smelling, which is not to be wondered at, considering that it is their custom to smear their bodies with butter and grease, and that they generally put on a new layer without removing the former one. But suddenly, as if by some enchantment, we saw them disappear in all directions, and we were left alone in the middle of a court.

Their precipitate flight was soon explained by the appearance of the Grand Lama. He was proceeding to a temple near by, crowned with a yellow hat resembling an old Roman helmet in shape, and had in his hand a painted wooden sceptre. He has the right to inflict severe corporal chastisement on any lamas whom he may find offending as he passes along, and the latter are not at all anxious to meet him.

He was a cheerful looking person, of the well-fed type, and he allowed us to photograph him with evident pleasure. The Kumbum lamas have been completely civilised by the passing visits and sojournings of a few Europeans, and have even learnt the value of tips.

What we particularly wanted to see was the famous tree which is attributed by legend to the times of the Buddha himself, and on whose leaves and bark letters like those in the Buddhist books are supposed to appear, which are universally venerated and worshipped. Some travellers have attached great value to this legend, and assert that the phenomena of the appearance of the letters cannot be otherwise explained. We never imagined for a moment that anything supernatural took place, and our only object was to discover the "fake" practised by the lamas to inflame to such an extent the credulity of the pilgrims. In December the tree, a kind of wild cherry, was naturally leafless, but the priest in charge of the temple before which it grows begged us to admire the lettering printed on the bark, which only extended, a point worth noting, to the height of a man. Its falsehood was not difficult to determine, and to make sure I inscribed my name in Chinese characters, according to the process evidently employed.

A thin transparent skin covers the bark of the tree, loose in places, and hanging along the trunk. Between this and the bark is a certain amount of liquid which colours the skin. If the skin is forcibly pressed against the bark the liquid is forced aside, and the skin sticks to the bark by atmospheric pressure. Owing to the absence of the liquid, a white line forms where the skin has been crushed, which can be seen some way off.

This is how the writing grows on the famous tree at Kumbum. The tree itself also is far from being very ancient.

I had hardly finished writing my name when the lamas who were present became violently angry and pushed us out of the enclosure with more energy than consideration, while the priest in charge of the sacred tree prostrated himself before the altar at the back of the little temple, and began a series of noisy prayers and exorcisms. However, we got back to our lodging in peace, followed by an unsympathetic crowd, and, having bought a few curiosities, we set out on our return journey to Sining-fu by a shorter road than that by which we had come, across the small group of hills to the north-east.

One of the greatest difficulties that the traveller in China has to contend with is the unpunctuality of the people that he has to employ. And the worst of it is that there is no remedy for it; for in the primitive intellect of the peasants, mule-drivers, and members of the lower classes, the notion of time is extremely vague. In spite of our orders to the people we had hired for our journey to Liang-chou, across the lofty and difficult mountain country named after Czar Alexander III., to be punctual at six o'clock in the morning, not one had deigned to put in an appearance at ten o'clock, and I was beginning to lose patience when at length our drivers and their animals came in under the gateway of the inn.

We had had great difficulty in securing the necessary transport. The way was hard, and even perilous in winter, and no one was anxious to venture upon it, considering that it is possible to reach Liang-chou almost comfortably by the Ping-fan road. But this latter well-known road was not what we wanted, and although the season was against us, we had determined to go by the mountain way, and to overcome with high pay the reluctance of the mule-owners. Furthermore, the inhabitants of these mountains have a very bad reputation. Rightly or wrongly, they are said to plunder and rob travellers without mercy, and our own servants trembled in every limb at the thought of the great perils, from men and from nature, which they were about to experience.

We soon entered a valley, through which ran a small half-frozen stream, the general direction of which was clearly north. The slope was gentle, the ground firm, and after a quick march of 22 miles, we reached the small town of Wan-yuen-fu at nightfall, where we had to put up for the night at the most disgusting kon-kuan imaginable. On the 12th of December we managed to get the men up early, and started at sunrise. The view was then a lovely one. We were in the centre of a small plateau covered with snow like a thick and spotless carpet. The walls of the town, as we left them, were hidden by snow, and the high peaks before us were snow-capped. The cold was nipping, below zero at seven o'clock; but luckily the wind had not yet risen and a sharp walk rapidly warmed us.

The march of the day before had been easy; that day's was not. My men tried one last effort to make us return to Sining-fu and take the Ping-fan road. They knelt down in the snow, and, with grotesque gestures of despair, once more described to us the dangers ahead.

They had met a soldier, they said, who had come over the same road in winter two years before, and lost his mules and his baggage.

To put an end to these lamentations, I bade them bring up the soldier. He was a tall and insolent ruffian. As he began to repeat his string of lies I struck him across the face with my riding-whip and sent him rolling in the snow. I promised similar treatment to any one who should make any further reference to the perils of crossing the Alexander III. Mountains, perils which I considered infinitesimal myself.

We began to climb, and the slope was at times steep enough to make it necessary for us to urge our animals on. The people of the country are the ancient aboriginals of Kansu, the most authentic survivors of the primitive race, from which the Chinese have sprung. The type is by no means savage or brutish; on the contrary, it appears to bear a stamp of refinement and good humour. They are easily distinguishable from the ordinary Chinese by their finer features, the size of their eyes, and their simple look. The head-dress of the women is distinctly like that of the ladies of Tibet in shape; but they wear no ornaments or jewels.

These people are obviously very poor and very hardy. Some among them were simply attired in old sacks, and the young children played about almost naked in piercing cold, which forced us to draw our fur cloaks closely round us.

Having crossed two fairly easy ridges, we came down again into a valley running from north to south, above which rose the loftiest ridge that we had to negotiate. The country round was practically desert. Only one poor dilapidated house could be made out, on our right. The savage aspect was impressive, the more so that the path which we were following was almost wholly concealed, the mules and horses leaving no tracks on the pebbly soil. The river, or rather the torrent, was frozen, and large blocks of ice here and there showed where the water had tried to force its way. In the valley a large amount of flint and granite of all colours was noticeable. I counted seven different tints of stone, sometimes in layers, and producing an unusual and picturesque effect.

The climb became more and more difficult, and, shortly before reaching the summit of the pass, the frozen snow on the ground, made slippery by the tread of our animals, made the march a dangerous one. I determined accordingly to alight, not feeling safe on the old mule that I was riding. I had hardly walked 50 yards when the animal suddenly fell and slipped on its back some little distance without hurting itself much. It was suffering from mountain sickness, although we were not at a height of 12,000 feet, and we had to carry it on the slippery slope.

At the top of the pass I gave the straining caravan a rest, and consulted the barometer and thermometer. We had risen nearly 3,000 feet since the morning, and the glass stood at 4° below zero, although we were in brilliant sunshine. Unfortunately there was a strong wind, and we could not think of resting for long.

Then we began a descent on the northern side of the pass, which was really dangerous, and such as I had not contemplated. The slope was exceedingly steep, and the winding path which followed it entirely covered with ice. Every one wondered how the mules were going to get down without losing their footing and taking "headers" into the abyss.

The caravan started off, using every possible precaution. For fear the men might be dragged away by the animals, I ordered the latter to be left free to make the descent in their own way. Strange as this may seem, I had absolute confidence in the admirable balancing instinct of the mule, a confidence which has never been shaken. So the animals went down impelled by the weight of their loads, squatting on their hind legs, slipping rapidly down the frozen slope. Sometimes they cannoned into one another, and their loads became entangled; but they always managed to retain their balance at the last moment with marvellous agility, even when they seemed lost.

As for ourselves, we followed in a more dignified manner. Sometimes walking and sometimes—otherwise. We had removed our smooth leather shoes, which would have added to the danger, and were marching in woollen socks, with the result that our feet soon became as cold as the ice we were treading, and caused us much pain. To add to the charm of the situation, it was growing dark, and the bottom of the gorge became absolutely indistinct. We could not see the mules, which had distanced us considerably.

At length the slope became easier and the path wider. The ice which covered it was less thick, and we could increase our pace and search for the animals which we soon discovered, huddled on the frozen ground, exhausted by their efforts during the descent. To the great astonishment of the men, not one mule was hurt, and not one load damaged. As it was out of the question to pass the night in this spot, we went on in the hope of reaching a small inn we had been told of about 5 miles from the pass. We arrived there at eleven o'clock, having crossed the icy water of several large torrents, and after many tumbles over the stones and rocks which filled the road, and could not be distinguished in the thick darkness.

Then we had to wake the inn-keeper, who was asleep, and make our way through the bales of all kinds which blocked the entrance of the only room. A fire was lighted with great difficulty, which filled the room with smoke rather than heat, and under these sorry circumstances we passed the night.

We started again early the next morning in spite of the grumbling of the mule-drivers, who wanted to make us spend a day in this dirty house, under the pretence of giving the animals a rest. The real reason was that being paid by the day they lost no opportunity of trying to increase the sum that would be due to them at the end of the journey. The first few miles led us along a little path which was slippery with glazed frost, and wound along by the side of the river, sometimes clinging to the rocks, and sometimes by the water's edge. The valley gradually widened, and pine trees appeared, which made the desolate country look more cheerful. The slope was fairly steep, and the torrent ran at great speed in its bed, which accounted for its not being frozen. This road must be absolutely impassable when the snows melt, owing to the height and force of the waters.

During the night the temperature had stood at 10° below zero, but in this enclosed valley, where we were sheltered from the wind, the influence of a glorious sun soon made itself felt, and towards midday the temperature was about

34°. In the evening the gorge was perceptibly wider, scattered cottages were to be seen, and we met convoys of tiny asses carrying pine logs to Tien-tan-tzeu. One end of the log was attached to the pack-saddle, and the other trailed on the ground. These little donkeys can in this manner convey loads of several hundredweight from one place to another.

Soon the torrent, the right bank of which we had been following, joined a river, and we were close to the lamasery of Tien-tan-tzeu, the white walls of which we detected at a turn of the road after crossing a bridge which was strikingly constructed of beams of wood laid one upon another, each one-third larger than that immediately below it. A little further we had to cross the river, and, as at this point the current was less rapid, and the bed of the river wider and more level, the frost had had time to do its work, and the water was covered with a thick coating of ice which acted as a natural bridge. The solidity of this did not seem to me beyond suspicion, as we occasionally heard prolonged sounds of cracking, and on close examination I discovered that as the level of the water had perceptibly fallen the current was no longer supporting the weight of the ice, but was running at a distance of a foot or so below it. However, we had no choice but to go on. I ordered the mules to be sent over one by one in spite of their plainly manifested terror. I was hoping that we should achieve our end without running any serious risk, when I observed that two of my caravan men, no doubt finding it tedious to wait until the mules and drivers that preceded them had singly reached the other bank in safety, were trying to make a single journey of the crossing, not only for themselves, but for three heavily laden mules with them. In spite of repeated orders they continued to advance, and we saw with horror the ice swaying in a most disquieting fashion beneath their weight. There was a crack, and a fissure appeared, but by some extraordinary chance the elasticity of the ice still held out for a few minutes, and these reckless fellows arrived safely, half dead with fright, and promptly received the due punishment of their disobedience.

When we reached the lamasery we were taken to a house which was luckily newly built. It was remarkably clean, and lacked the peculiar smell which the Mongols and Tibetans have an unfortunate habit of imparting to any house in which they stay. Pinewood wainscoting adorned the rooms and, which was a really wonderful thing, the door shut quite fast. The chief lamas did not put in an appearance. This fortunate fact enabled us to dine early, and to enjoy a well-earned meal without first having to run the gauntlet of their curious questionings.

On leaving the lamasery next day we took the road to the north-west, which followed for some time the course of the river which we had crossed the day before on the ice, at a height of some hundred feet above it.

As I was jogging along behind the caravan, admiring the snow-covered country, which was really surprisingly magnificent, an enormous eagle suddenly dashed out of the rocks and swept on extended wings close to my mule's head. The animal taking fright leaped to the edge of the abyss, and for a second I felt myself hopelessly lost. Two of its hoofs lost their hold on the path and kicked loose stones down on to the ice below. But by a great effort of its steel-like muscles it recovered its hold, and the incident was miraculously over, leaving us safe and sound. My nerves were so shaken by the horrible tension of that second that I felt I could ride no more on that stage, and preferred to walk to the end of it.

On this day we saw every kind of game, pheasants, wild peacocks of an uncommon slaty blue colour, stags, and antelopes. The pheasants especially were countless, and furnished us with an excellent stock of provisions. All day long we were climbing ridges, only coming down into valleys to climb again.

The differences of altitude reached sometimes 1,200 or 1,600 feet, and wearied the caravan animals. This was no doubt the reason why the mule-drivers tried to deceive us, and to make an attempt to take the Ping-fan road without my noticing it. But I discovered the plan, and their trickery only resulted in their being fined to the extent of some *taels*. Towards evening the road passed a coal mine which was being worked, near the top of a ridge, in an imposing and wild situation. Some miners were living at an altitude of 9,900 feet, working their mine when the atmospheric conditions allowed them. A little lower down discharges of gas made us cough. This was escaping from some narrow clefts on the side of the mountain, and going on we came to a spring of warm water containing iron and carbon, the steam of which rose in a column condensed by the bitterly cold air. The water came out of the earth at a temperature of 85°.

Our lodging for the night at Trahou was less poor and dilapidated than we had feared, a peasant's inn, surrounded by some fields, at the bottom of a valley running north and south, but the next day was another weary and back-breaking climb. The first pass was 3,300 feet above the level of Chantou. Luckily none were covered with snow like that which we had crossed on the 12th, and they were easily negotiated. Not a living soul came in sight. All was wild desert. In the evening we reached Ra-liou-tua-tse quite worn out. From this village to Liang-chou the road became easy, continually descending, and the ground, though frozen, was not too slippery. We reached Liang-chou on the 20th of December without any further adventures worth recording.

CHAPTER VI

TOWARDS REPALARAITSE

LIANG-CHOU is a comparatively well-known city. Not only have some European explorers visited it, such as Bonin and Sven Hedin, but two missions are flourishing there in healthy rivalry. One is a Belgian Catholic Mission, with a good number of converts, the other is a station of the China Inland Mission, richer in hope than in achievement.

The city is a detestable one, not only because of the evil smells which abound in it, but much more owing to the character of the people in Northern Kansu. In no country is human intelligence so dense and slow as here. Such, at least, was the opinion of Confucius. The slightest undertaking, the most slender purchase, takes an infinite time, and usually turns out unsuccessful. The Mandarins were polite to us, but really hostile, as is always the case in mission stations. The people have no respect for Europeans, and these are frequently insulted in broad daylight, since certain missionaries allow themselves to be abused without replying.

The city itself is large, even too large for the population and for the number of houses made of mud and pebbles which are in it. It is built on the broad strip of land which stretches across Northern Kansu, between the mountains and the Gobi.

We happened to put up at the temple of Shi-lai-seu, or the temple dedicated to the man coming from the East. For the time that we had to spend in Liang-chou during our preparations for an expedition into the unknown Gobi, we preferred its rooms, recently whitewashed for the mining agents of the King of the Belgians, to an inn.

Our object was to identify certain lakes printed in a dubious manner on the map, whose existence was alleged by some, and denied by others; but on learning that we were going to penetrate into a country practically unknown, my caravan drivers from San-tao-ho, who had never shown any taste for a life of adventure, cried aloud, and swore by all their gods that they all had extremely aged parents or children of a tender age, who required looking after without delay. I dismissed them all, without any regret, for greater liars and sluggards I had never met; and I set about finding new servants.

This was no easy task, for the people of Liang-chou have the reputation of being shameless robbers, and, if possible, I wanted only to employ safe men. The best course was to approach the Belgian missionaries, who since they knew many families could recommend the most likely and the least dishonest persons. With their aid I got together a sufficient number of men; but then a great difficulty arose. These gentlemen were willing to go with us wherever we wished to venture, provided that we did not leave the high road! The efforts and diplomacy which were necessary to get them to start for the unknown would fill a book. One, having promised, changed his mind next day. Another was held back by his wife, another by his children, a fourth by his mill. The truth was that they had a great fear that we should all perish together.

None the less we set out on the 4th of January 1905 with a staff shaking in its shoes, and on which no reliance could be placed. Our caravan included twenty-five camels, which had remained in pretty bad condition, in spite of Lao Yang's promises at Ping-fan, and one riding-horse. Four men drove the camels, and at evening had to pitch the Mongol tent given us by the King of Alashan. A fellow of strange character and grotesque appearance had undertaken the responsibilities of the kitchen, and a tall, disconnected young man acted as valet and butler.

Our provisions for a three months' journey included all that we could obtain in this badly-supplied city. We carried with us, in great grey sacks upon our camels, 700 lbs. of flour, 250 lbs. of millet, 200 lbs. of rice, 100 lbs. of meat, which we trusted the frost to preserve, and 1,000 lbs. of peas for the animals, to sustain them during the several days in succession, when they would find no green food.

A strip of cultivated land stretches along the banks of the Poua River from Liang-chou to Lake Tching-trou-rou, the first of the sheets of water which we wished to identify; but, instead of following the winding water-courses, we decided to cut across the desert and to meet the river again at the small town of Chen-fan, where dwells the Mandarin charged with the government of the Emperor's subjects who have settled in this remote portion of the Empire. For two days we crossed fields of various crops, in the middle of which from time to time rose farms with high fortified walls. The country was unquestionably fertile, well watered by the streams which come down from the mountains, and drained automatically by the natural slope of the ground towards the desert, so as to spread the water where it is wanted for fertilisation.

We crossed the Poua on our third day's march. The swiftness of its current, though it has not much water in summer, had preserved it from being entirely frozen, but blocks of ice which were carried down it bumped against the legs of our quiet camels.

The temperature at this season, although very cold, was extremely pleasant. The sun rose and sank every day in a cloudless sky, and if, during the night, the temperature often fell 20° below zero, by day it was sometimes so hot that we had to unbutton our thick sheepskin cloaks. Towards evening, as a rule, we had a light breeze from the north-west.

But we soon passed the lines of cultivation, and began to traverse the great plain, grassy and deserted, interrupted by ridges of sand. After 7 miles, we came upon the small deserted temple of La-pa-tchoui, built upon a little rise in the ground, below which are two springs, which were then transformed by the frost into two pools of ice. The temple is surrounded by ruins, and the great wall here takes a turn northward. We crossed the wall twice on our march towards the north, and on the other side of its remains we pursued our way over a great rolling plain, well covered with grass even at that season, in which troops of antelopes were roaming.

Before we had left Liang-chou more than five days, the courage of our drivers began to fail. On the morning of the 9th January two men begged me to let them return to their dear Liang-chou, alleging a sudden illness, of which they showed no symptoms, for they were two hardy fellows gifted with splendid appetites. Naturally, I did not grant their request; but to avoid a recurrence of these fancy ailments I made them swallow large doses of ipecacuanha. This made them think twice before trying a fresh subterfuge.

We lost this day altogether, for my horse,

the only one we had, having bolted, we were employed until sunset in recapturing him.

As we went on, we found that the grassy plateau was succeeded by a sandy plain covered with small stones, on the left some low, bare hills, and across the plain itself some furrows in the sand. There was absolutely no green food here, and as I did not wish to encroach upon our stock of peas, I resorted for the nourishment of the caravan to a convoy of peasants who were going from Chen-fan to Kan-chou, carrying to the latter town a large supply of straw and forage. At a high price we obtained what we wanted, as these poor beggars saw in our difficulty a means of making a large profit.

Next day, after crossing two large frozen rivers, the Ta-Si-Ho and the Siao-Si-Ho, whose frozen beds were hardly roads designed for camels, and a smaller river, the To-Ho-Tse, we left the sand, and after 11 miles, were glad to reach country well cultivated and thickly inhabited. The lines of the fields were broken only by occasional banks of sand carried by violent spring winds.

A further march of 8 miles brought us under the walls of the town of Chen-fan, half buried in the sand, and sheltering a collection of extremely wretched mud-huts. There is no kon-kuan in this town, which is the terminus of Chinese administration towards the desert, and no Mandarin, except the sub-prefect in charge, ever ventures into this neighbourhood. We had, therefore, to pitch our Mongol tent in the court of a dusty inn, whose rooms were some of them roofless, and others without doors, in a temperature of 25° below zero.

Just before we reached the town, Han, our valet, having mounted against all orders on an already loaded camel, and having gone to sleep on it, pleasantly rocked by the pitching and rolling which makes the boldest sea-sick, had fallen from his mount on to the ice, and had dislocated his knee. Accordingly, I called the most fashionable humbug at Chen-fan to his help, promising a good reward if the tibia and femur of our servant, who wept like a child, should be properly set. The doctor got to work at once, and began by filling his mouth with warm water, which he then discharged on his patient's knee. After ten minutes of this treatment, he went through a series of gestures, worthy of the most accomplished charlatan, and only then did he set the injured knee. The performance took a long time, but the result was satisfactory.

I had learnt from experience never to interfere myself in serious cases. The European, who is foolishly kind enough to try to minister to the woes of others, gains as his only sign of gratitude a charge of having tried to poison the patient, if his remedies have not full effects, and has to bear upon his shoulders the responsibility of all the evils experienced by the sufferer.

North of Chen-fan, the Russian maps, which are the best for all that concerns the Gobi, mark an absolute desert. We were therefore prepared for a march over sand and stones, guided only by the compass and the sextant, and were much surprised to travel for three days, for a distance of over 50 miles, through cultivated fields, and to meet continually with large farms, the whole country being intersected by irrigation canals carrying the fertilising water of the Poua-Ho and its tributaries.

The road was good, and would have been practicable for carts. The river ran on our left with cultivation on one side of it, and the rocky and sandy desert on the other.

The natural slope of the ground has only permitted irrigation of the land on the right bank. The country was flat, and sparsely-wooded, and the sun poured down blinding beams. On the 14th of January we made no march. We were at the village of Tching-trou-rou, on the actual edge of the desert, and as the pack-saddles of the camels were in very bad condition, had decided to spend a day in mending them. The *cul de sac* in which we were was surrounded by sand on all sides. Chinese cultivation ended here, and we could not be far away from the Tching-trou-rou Lake, which takes its name from the village, and into which the Poua-Ho flows. We had crossed the river once more the evening before, and for the future it lay on our right.

On the morrow, having crossed the sand ridges

THE CARAVAN IN THE SANDS NEAR TCHING-TROU-ROU.

[*To face p.* 166.

without much trouble, we reached a large plain encircled by bare rocky mountains, which looked mauve in the distance. There was no sign of the presence of any lake, and we moved by intuition towards a cleft which was indicated in the mountains in front. There were many antelopes in the district which were not very wild, and I had several shots at them. This led us to observe a most interesting phenomenon. The cartridges of the Mannlicher rifle, loaded with cordite, carrying ordinarily more than 2,000 yards, exploded with an altogether different sound from their usual dry crack, and the bullets fell spent, with a wide trajectory, at 150 or 200 yards. We could only attribute this to the intense cold to which the cartridges were exposed. Had we been attacked then, our defence would have been very feeble—we could not have relied upon the range of our rifles, or the accuracy of our aim.

Towards evening our attention was attracted to a white mass on the right, and I felt sure that we were not far from the lake, the ice on which could be perceived. We inclined eastward, and, soon after, reached the banks of the lake. Two poor cottages stood near by, marking the site of a well at which we were to spend the night. The water of the lake happened to be slightly salt, and unfit to drink or to use in cooking.

On the border of the lake dead fish already dried showed that the water-level had sunk since the spring flood, and 100 yards from the edge masses of thick ice broken and forced up proved that the sinking had gone on since the first days of frost. I could not determine the shape of the lake, which was surrounded on the south-east and north-east by huge ridges of sand, and on the west and north by a plain and some bare hills. All its lines were confused by an intense mirage, a glittering of the white mass of the ice, and of the reflection of the sand. The inhabitants of the huts at Seu roung nou tien asserted that the circuit of the lake was 200 *lis*; but this estimate seemed to me an exaggerated one.

The next day we set out across the sand to the north-east of the lake; we had never seen such high ridges, and at first I thought the caravan would never get out of them. There were real precipices between them, sometimes more than 90 feet deep, where the wind collected, whilst over our heads it picked up the dry sand and spread it over the caravan in a thin rain. The displacement of the sand here must be very rapid, for having ordered a halt of some minutes, in the course of this back-breaking journey over the yielding ground, I noticed that, 100 yards behind us, in the very track of our caravan, the wind had heaped up a layer of sand more than a foot thick.

After painful efforts maintained for several hours we got out of this *impasse*, which on a stormy day would certainly entomb any rash adventurers.

A little later we reached the summit of a crest of lava, which commanded the lake. These beds of lava stretched from the north-west to the south-east for a distance of at least several miles. They are now as high as the summits around them; but it cannot have been so in old times, for while the wind and the sand have levelled the rocks on the top of the mountains and reduced them to a uniform height, they have left the lava ridges untouched.

Then we found to our great astonishment that the lake Tching-trou-rou is composed of two sheets of water separated by a narrow isthmus which the sand can open or block in a short time. The smaller sheet, entirely hidden by the sand-hills, is shallow, and lies to the north of the other.

Having crossed the lava ridges, we lost sight of the lake and of the whole basin through which we had been marching for several days. We sighted a small valley full of a coarse grass, which, although dried by the frost, made excellent food for the animals, and we decided to halt there. The water we were carrying with us in the form of ice made it unnecessary to search for a well, and camels can spend long days without drinking, especially in winter.

We were about to cross the sheer desert, whose long desolate furrows impress forcibly the strongest mind and the most self-confident of men. It is not a matter of nerves, but simply the distinct knowledge that, while crossing these huge dead expanses, a caravan's existence is at the mercy of any accident that cannot be foreseen, and of any mistake in the calculation of longitude and latitude which may result in an inability to find water and supplies.

Even the faintest trace of a path had altogether disappeared. The neighbourhood was painfully monotonous, the horizon was bounded on all sides by a chain of low hills wrapped in a bluish mist in which, as in mirage, they seemed to move. The men presented an appearance even more disconsolate than that of Nature, for they seemed to have lost all hope, and performed their duties with even less energy than usual.

We marched all day over the desert extending on all sides, in the manner that I have described, for several hundred miles. About 60 miles to the west, a great chain of mountains, Yapala-shan, stretched its blue-grey mass, whose lines were confused and lost under the rays of the burning sun. The march itself was as simple as possible. There were no obstacles to turn us from our straight course, and when we stopped for the night near the well of Mona Shanse, which we had some difficulty in finding, since the man we had engaged as a guide did not know the way, and had never really visited the district, we had covered 15 miles almost without noticing them. As the readers will be able to judge in the course of my narrative, the halt nearly proved fatal to one of us—but I must not anticipate events.

On the 19th of January we set out again under intense cold aggravated by a cutting wind. We had hardly covered a mile before the course of our guide became even more erratic than on the day before, and having questioned him closely I made him admit that he did not know towards which of the three heights which stood out to the north we ought to be making. Accordingly I resumed control of the caravan, and to the great surprise of our people gave the order to incline to the left, and to make for a depression which was indicated in the Yapalashan. If the Russian map was correct, there should be here a little Mongol temple visited some years before by a Russian explorer, where I hoped to find a better qualified guide. I calculated that we were about 35 miles from it.

A stretch of yellow sand lay in front of us, with ridges which did not look high, but foreboded a total absence of water. So I ordered the head camel driver, Lao Yang, to go back to the wells, and to fill some of the casks, while we went on slowly.

He did not seem pleased at the order, for he took some time to get started. We thought that he would recover from his sulks, and would faithfully perform my instructions, and his ill-will gave us no further anxiety. We were the more astonished when he joined us again after another 13 miles at finding the casks empty and hearing him explain that our habit of trusting to chance displeased him, and that he had not procured any water, so as to force us to retrace our steps. We were therefore obliged to camp on the sand, and to wait up to a late hour of the night the return of two camel drivers, whom I hastily despatched to the wells. Lao Yang was a little too sore to go himself.

I admit that we had begun to have some doubts as to the success of this expedition, supported as we were by a head servant of the type of Lao Yang, disobedient, arrogant, and untruthful, and by others terrified at the stories of death from thirst which he had repeated to them ever since we started. These men could never understand how I was able to lead them straight from point to point merely by observing the stars. They could only see in my orders the frightful symptoms of an insanity of which they were to be the victims.

On the following day we crossed small ridges of sand all some 10 feet high, and running from north to south. It was only towards evening that we reached a slightly different site, where some alpic bushes afforded food to the camels—which they needed badly.

From the tent door we could see clearly the depression towards which I had led the caravan, and which proved to be a broad pass cutting the mountain chain in two.

We reached the temple of Kush late next day,

in a snowstorm, which hid the leading animals of the caravan from the men in the rear. This fall of snow made the cold less bitter, and gave an Arctic appearance to the whole district, which was covered by a spotless white mantle which crackled under the heavy tread of the camels.

The temple, inhabited by a small number of lamas, has no striking peculiarity. It is built near a well to the side of the road taken by the numerous caravans which carry the trade between Kwei-hua-cheng and Kan-chou-fu, by way of Paotu and Repalaraitse. This road passes somewhat to the south-east of the great temple of Aque-miao. All along its course are small pagodas, like those of Kush, in which a few miserable monks vegetate without even the resource, in this awful desert, of cattle-breeding, like some of their more fortunate colleagues. They spend their time in begging a little money or food from the caravan drivers, and live for long years on this barren ground, only passing from their smoky and dusty rooms to the cold and dark hall of the temple, in which they mutter indefinitely prayers which they do not understand.

These wretched people would very soon die of hunger, but for the superstitious credulity of the caravan drivers, who imagine that the lamas can throw an evil spell over their beasts, or, which is more likely, poison the well, and destroy their pack animals.

The snow continued to fall for two days, and,

as marching under these conditions was really very painful, we remained stationary. I was suffering also from a slight attack of fever, for which complete rest was the best cure. But our life under our felt tent was very dull and monotonous. The day gave us hardly light enough to read by, and no noise broke the silence as of the grave. The wind had dropped, and the carpet of snow deadened the footfall of the caravan drivers.

When we started again on 25th January, we followed the road which I mentioned before. This, being thickly covered with snow, was hard to find. A few days would see us at Repalaraitse, the point at which the roads of the Gobi Desert meet, at right angles.

Towards evening there was a fresh fall of snow; the ground was covered to the depth of a foot, and after a short march, we pitched our tent. All day we met no one, and the tracks of our caravan on the snow were blotted out under the fresh fall, like the wake of a ship. The death-like stillness of the huge expanses seemed never to be broken by the noise and bustle of life.

For three days we journeyed in the same direction to the north-east, now mounting and now descending the long and gentle slope, between two ranges of bare hills, far distant and low. The country was mournful and deserted looking when the sky was cloudy; but when the sun shone upon the huge white plain the sight was magnificent, though rather blinding to the eyes.

IN THE GOBI DESERT, NEAR REPALARAITSE

[To face p. 174.

We were only a few miles from Repalaraitse, and in view of the last hill that conceals the temple, when our march northward was arrested by one of those accidents against which the will of man can do nothing.

My wife, who so far had borne the fatigue of this long journey excellently, was attacked by typhoid fever. The readers will remember my statement that the well of Mona Shanse was to prove fatal to us.

The water of this well had been poisoned by decayed bones and morsels of skin and flesh from camels which had died of weariness or disease. Unluckily we had only discovered this too late. It was more than enough to develop the germs of this dreadful disease. Accordingly we had to stay at this desolate place covered with snow for twenty-two days, without drinking water, except such as we could obtain by melting the snow, and without any means of renewing our provisions, which were gradually diminishing. We wondered anxiously what we should do when they were entirely exhausted. I had brought food for three months, but had not reckoned on the careless gluttony of the men, who ate twice as much as they needed, or on the wear and tear of the sacks which were never mended, and which allowed their precious contents to be scattered on the march.

During this lapse of time, which seemed as though it would never end, the temperature was very cold, frequently dropping to 37° below zero.

There was no fresh snow, and the sky recovered its splendid clearness, but great hurricane winds blowing from the west penetrated all the clefts of our tent, and made our situation almost intolerable.

Some long caravans of thin camels travelling from Paotu to Kan-chou-fu passed close to us. They moved slowly one after another, two or three hundred in number, many of them carrying on their necks bells, whose mournful tinkling echoed across the great flats, in a manner which we shall long remember.

I often tried to buy such provisions as rice and peas from these passing caravan drivers, but they would not sell them at any price, being themselves sadly impoverished, and having no more than they needed for their own support.

At last the day came when we had to think of returning to Liang-chou at once, although my poor invalid wife had by no means recovered. We had rations for only three days, and the camels had for some days had nothing to eat except the thin brushwood which appeared here and there above the snow, and which we also used for fuel.

One of the questions which exercised me most was as to how these wretched animals would be able to take us back to our starting-point, exhausted as they were by want of food.

We hastily constructed a litter of poor materials, which broke down more than once on the way, and set out on the 20th of February, not knowing whether we should reach Liang-chou in time, since all depended on a specially rapid march, which it seemed hard to expect from the caravan animals.

However, the day before, I had visited Repalaraitse, where a temple stands to the south of a moderate-sized lake. This temple and its lamas are richer than usual, for a number of roads meet here. They are as follows: from Paotu to Kan-chou, from Paotu to Chen-fan, from Paotu to Moming, from Fu-ma-fu to Moming, from Fu-ma-fu to Uliassutai, from Fu-ma-fu to Khamil. The number of camel caravans that pass this place is considerable, and sometimes a score of them encamp side by side on the banks of the lake, since there is a sufficiency of grass in the neighbourhood. The Gobi Desert is, as a matter of fact, more productive in these places, than is generally supposed. Some stretches are certainly an absolute desert, covered with dry and shifting sand, or fine gravel, but here and there are meeting-places in which one feels closer to China and less lost.

I will say little of the anxiety of the return journey. We accomplished marches so long and tedious that they were really achievements. Many of our camels were unable to keep up, and the caravan was much reduced, both in men and animals, when we reached Liang-chou.

Fortunately we met with no accidents, and the

men we had left behind us joined us again at Liang-chou safe and well after a short rest.

Miss Mellor, a lady of the China Inland Mission, nursed my wife with skill and devotion, for which we shall ever be specially grateful. Little by little she was restored to health, and was again eager to continue the journey which had been so unhappily interrupted.

CHAPTER VII

FROM LIANG-CHOU TO AN-SI-CHOU. PREPARATION FOR TIBET

On the 5th of May we started again for the town of Yung Thrung, from which we proposed to make an expedition into the desert to look for another lake, marked on some maps, of which the inhabitants of the country professed complete ignorance. From this lake we intended to go to Moming, and thence to An-si-chou, all the while remaining inside the Gobi. In this latter town, almost on the borders of the Northern Kansu, we should complete our caravan and buy the necessary provisions for our crossing of Tibet from north to south. The route was entirely new, and crossed only country unknown to Europeans.

We left Liang-chou in rain, a light spring rain which would last all day, and we reached Yung Thrung in two days. Our road crossed valleys formed by water-courses in the mass of loess, pebbles, and earth brought down from the great southern mountains. Some important passes are to be found in this chain, which all, more or less, lead towards Sining-fu. One of them is inhabited by some people called Sifins, who have a bad reputation, and gave some trouble to the explorer Bonin.

On the 8th of May we left Yung Thrung early, hoping to reach Ning-yüan-pu before night, and plunged into a mountain defile, following the banks of the river Ta Ho (great river), which does not deserve this pompous name. All day long we travelled northward, cutting across ridges of hills running from east to west, all uninhabited, and containing, I think, many minerals. Towards the middle of the afternoon, at a place called Ho-si-pu, we found a long broad plain fairly well cultivated, and covered with farms. The Great Wall again put in an appearance there, in the shape of a moderate mound of earth, and all the dwellings had lofty towers abundantly fortified with stones and pebbles. Having marched another 7 miles we reach Ning-yüan-pu just as the sun was setting.

Ning-yüan-pu is a picturesque little town on the right bank of the Ta Ho, with no great commerce or industry. It serves as a rallying point for the farmers and peasants scattered over this remote corner of China. A worm-eaten wooden bridge, on which no heavy load dare pass, leads up to it. Opposite the town, on a cone-shaped hill, stands a large number of small red and white pagodas dedicated to the genii of the desert, the wind, and the rain. Beyond Ning-yüan-pu lies the bare desert, sinking perceptibly towards the north, in which the Ta Ho apparently disappears. The mountain ends at Ning-yüan-pu, but one chain extends towards the north-west, of which I shall speak again.

We wished to follow the course of the Ta Ho, and enquired what became of it. Accordingly, leaving on our right a road which leads to Chen-fan, we set out across a dry and barren country, the soil of which, being made of pebbles, was firm under foot. We had been informed at Ning-yüan-pu that a series of villages, named Tien-su-Kiang and Chang-ning-hu had been built on a stretch of fertile alluvial ground in the heart of the desert about 20 miles to the north. We soon beheld them, twinkling in the distant mirage, since nothing blocked our view and the day was clear.

Nothing is more curious and interesting to the traveller than to find flourishing life and prosperous cultivation where he only expected the barrenness of the Gobi. These villages are far from poor, and would be rich, but for the sand hurricanes, which, from time to time destroy some of their fields, and rob them of the profits of their labours. The water of the Ta Ho is skilfully used for the irrigation of the field, and herds of cows and camels feed peacefully around.

In answer to questions about the Ta Ho, the inhabitants of Tien-su-Kiang assured us that the river did not run on towards the north, but, on the contrary, took a turn to the east, and not far from Chen-fan joined the streams which pour into the lake Tching-trou-rou. We decided to verify this statement, and the next day reconnoitre the country to the north.

The Ta Ho did in fact change its course, and took a turn to the east, which would enable it to reach Chen-fan; but its volume was very much reduced, a large portion of its waters being drawn off for cultivation, and a great quantity being lost in the porous ground which here took the place of the gravel in the desert. In places there were great impassable stretches of mud, from which flowed little streams which united later on to form again the bed of the river. We saw no trace of a lake, except a pond made by human hands, and used for watering and bathing animals.

As we returned to Tien-su-Kiang (the most remote village), a terrible sand hurricane broke out. Immediately on all sides columns of whirling sand rose in the air, dragging after them all the small objects which they encountered. It was soon impossible to see even 2 or 3 yards ahead, and, as the wind still grew in violence our only course was to stretch ourselves on the ground with cloaks over our heads. I admired the patience of the Mongol horses. Accustomed from their youth to these natural hardships, they only turned their backs to the wind, and from time to time shook their ears when the pebbles struck them, though the violence of the wind now and again drove them some paces forward.

This hurricane lasted for about twenty minutes.

Then the sky became clear, while large masses of sand and dust could be seen travelling southwards. According to the inhabitants it was one of the feeblest hurricanes that one could experience. I shudder at the thought of what the others must be like. These hurricanes are called *bouranes* in Chinese Turkestan, where they cause fearful damage; so at least the explorers who have experienced them assert.

Two days later we were back at Ning-yüan-pu, and continued our march westward, leaving the bed of the Ta Ho to the south. Our road was crossed by many small torrents and river beds, all making for the Ta Ho. In these days they are only rarely filled with water during the rainy season; but the deep impression they have made in the land and the ravines that they have dug out prove beyond question that the rainfall, now very feeble over all this district, was formerly heavy. This observation applies not only to the route which we were then taking, but generally to all the north of Kansu and the south of the Gobi.

We continued marching westward for two days, now rising slightly towards the north, and again inclining perceptibly towards the south. The country is by no means barren, and the abundance and quality of the pasturage increased as we advanced. The grass was high, there was plenty of good water in the wells. There were large herds of cattle, horses, and camels, handed over to the inhabitants of this district, for the summer, by the city traders of Kan-chou and the surrounding country.

The peasants, who live on these wide plains crossed by high ridges, and marked on the map as sandy desert, do not indulge in agriculture, but are content with the modest profits which they make by acting as cattle-drovers. There are but few cottages, since ten men can overlook a wide stretch of ground.

In the evening of the second day we reached the little ancient garrison town, which bears the name of Sia-kru, and which in olden times was built up against the Great Wall. To the north of this town is an immense stretch of grassy plain.

From Sia-kru we had suddenly decided to make for Kan-chou-fu, for we had heard much talk of the importance and prosperity of that city. The road to it, which follows the old Great Wall in a gentle downward slope, is one of the largest in Kansu. It passes many large villages and small fortified towns. The country is well cultivated, and seems fertile.

Before reaching Kan-chou-fu, we crossed the sandy bed of the river Edsin Gol, which is very broad, and found ourselves suddenly in a very fertile district, abundantly watered by various tributaries and affluents of the river, very populous and full of life. As we advanced, the high walls of the town rose before us with a curtain of trees in front of them, and tall trees overtopping them from inside.

The first sight of the town is very pleasing, but, unfortunately, it does not stand a closer examination. In fact, while this town has the great advantage of being very shady, it pays for it by being built on the site of an ancient marsh, and, during the rainy season, it becomes a collection of unhealthy swamps. Even during the dry season there are sheets of water, sometimes of considerable size, inside the walls on all sides, and the inhabitants may be seen angling in the pools created by the rains at their very doors—a spectacle as amusing as it is uncommon.

No house in Kan-chou is conceited enough to hold itself erect. The ground is too soft to bear the weight, even of slender mud walls, for many years, and the buildings, which are incessantly being rebuilt, change their position at once, as if afflicted by perpetual earthquake. This state of affairs causes no anxiety to the inhabitants, who live in peaceful happiness, sheltered by roofs which may come down on their heads at any minute. Four hundred years ago Kan-chou occupied a much better position, but popular superstition, so powerful in China, moved it in consequence of some disaster, and erected it again in this unsuitable spot.

We spent some days in Kan-chou, during which I took the opportunity of increasing the number of mules and horses that we should employ for our crossing of Tibet. I recruited them right and left as chance offered. The mules of Northern Kansu, although moderate in size, have extraordinary staying power, and can cover long distances under a load of 200 lbs. on scanty nourishment, consisting almost entirely of dry straw. The price of the best of these pack mules seldom exceeds 40 *taels*. The horses are even cheaper, and, excluding fast amblers, excellent mounts can be obtained, at 20 or 30 *taels*.

Han, one of our men, was suddenly taken ill, and profited by the seizure to indulge in his favourite secret vice of opium. Unluckily for him, as I made my round one night I discovered this, and informed him that he must either go back to Liang-chou at once or give up smoking. He assured me that he was only smoking because he was ill, and that opium acted upon him as a sedative. He might as well have said an anæsthetic, for the man seemed absolutely senseless.

We left him behind us at Kan-chou for some days after our departure, hoping that he would return to Liang-chou. He was an idle and stupid fellow, and feeble in health, and we thought that perhaps the crossing of Tibet would be more than he could manage.

To reach Moming we plunged into a corner of the Gobi Desert, instead of following the high road explored some years previously by the great Russian traveller Obrotchieff. Moming is situated on the river Edsin Gol, and commands the stretch of cultivated land which reaches to the centre of the desert for some hundred *lis* on the two sides of that water-course, which ends in two important lakes, the Sokho Nor and Athum Nor.

The route that the caravan pursued for several days was very monotonous. We travelled between the bed of the Edsin Gol and the desert. Occasionally we passed small hills, the outlying points of more important ridges starting from the Gobi, all running from east to west.

After a six days' march, we reached, on the 29th May, some sand-hills, so high that those previously described to the north of the lake Tching-trou-rou were not to be compared with them. They extend for 7 miles in length, and a mile or two in breadth from north to south. The highest are collected in the south, and reach a height varying from 150 to 200 feet.

I shudder to think what a sandstorm, a *bourane*, would be like, if it raged between these ridges of sand so easily shifted and displaced even by a light breeze. Luckily, during our crossing, there was complete peace, and not a grain of sand was whirling in the air.

It was even oppressively hot. Although we had become accustomed to begin our marches before daylight, between two and three o'clock in the morning, we had not yet been able altogether to avoid the terrible radiance of the sun on the sand and the gravel, and our progress was painful. When we halted, towards eleven o'clock in the morning, both men and beasts had well earned their rest.

When these high ridges had been crossed without serious difficulty we came out again upon the river Edsin Gol, flowing here over a gravel-bed in the midst of a desert dotted with small oases. On all sides, east, north, and west, the view was bounded by a horizon of sand-hills.

Having followed the Edsin Gol for two days across a monotonous country in which, however, the poverty of the inhabitants seemed to increase, we reached the town of Moming, also known as Mo-mo and Ping-su-ing.

This wretched and tiny city did not answer to the description we had received of it.

It is useless to ask for information in China, your interlocutor will always reply in the affirmative, through sheer politeness, and because he wishes to please you and become popular. I had asked different people, on a score of occasions, about the resources of Moming, enquiring especially whether I should be able to obtain a fresh stock of provisions there. In spite of previous experience in similar circumstances, I had relied from their replies upon being able to buy at Moming many provisions, and even animals, with which I was unwilling to burden our caravan on leaving Liang-chou.

Unfortunately, there is only one shop in Moming, and that shop has nothing for sale. With great difficulty we obtained a little rice, and some peas with which I had to nourish the mules for some weeks, to get them into good condition before venturing into the deserts of Tibet. As to buying animals, it was hopeless. All the mules which people tried to sell at ridiculous prices were nearly twenty years old, and hopped on three legs. The camels were only skin and bones, and their wistful eyes told a long story of privations and ill-treatment.

I had no other choice, and had to buy five of these poor creatures. I hoped that a substantial diet of peas and good grass would quickly restore them to condition, and I was not entirely disappointed in my expectations.

There is no konkuan at Moming, and as the inns were repulsively dirty we calmly took up our quarters in the chief temple, to the great astonishment and amusement of the inhabitants of the town. On reaching it we found opium smokers settled in the temple itself, which removed any hesitation or doubt as to the profanation of the sacred place. The chief hall was lofty and airy, and much to be preferred to any luxury in view of the torrid heat which oppressed the town.

In the course of the two days that we spent here Han arrived from Kan-chou by the high road along the left hand of the Edsin Gol. He brought with him a boy of nineteen called Siao-d'gan, consumptive in appearance, feeble, and entirely devoid of those qualities of physical soundness which all the men, except Han, possessed. We wanted to dismiss this rickety gentleman at once, but he begged so hard, and affirmed so stoutly that he was used to hard work, that we took him with us. It was an unfortunate weakness on our part, for we had hardly entered Tibet when he began to be a burden to everybody, and he died of chest and heart troubles before the end of the journey.

Moming would be nothing but a village were it not for the peculiarity of its situation, as I explained before. The inhabitants assured us that for the past three years not a drop of rain had fallen in the district, and that the lack of provisions and the sorry condition of the beasts were due to this fact. But for the Edsin Gol, the country would be an appalling desert.

Three high roads meet here, one comes from Repalaraitse, another from Khamil, the third goes to Su-chou-fu. The road from Khamil passes to the east of a low range of mountains which is visible to the north-west of the town.

The evening before the day of our departure heavy rain fell for the first time for years, and caused a great sensation. Some well-disposed spirits attributed this sudden fructifying downpour to the fortunate influence of our presence, which was very good of them.

On the 2nd of June we nearly lost the whole caravan in less than a quarter of an hour, in crossing the Edsin Gol. The bed of this river consists of shifting sand, constantly moving, whose exact situation is accordingly very difficult to determine. The peasants and caravan drivers who have to cross it fix wooden stakes here and there to mark the passage. Unluckily for us, the current had carried away half of them, and the ford was only marked out for the first 100 yards. The whole breadth is about 250, and when we reached the middle of the stream, which was swift, if not deep, we suddenly discovered that our pack mules instead of advancing were gradually disappearing under water. Our horses began to do the same, and we only had time to slip from our saddles into the water, while the terrified drivers ran from one animal to another, as far as the shifty sand would permit, vainly striving to set them on their legs again. Only the camels reached the further bank without much difficulty, since their large flat feet did not penetrate into the sand or the liquid mud. The mules, horses, and asses, continued to sink.

Luckily the river was not more than 2 feet deep, and when the poor beasts had sunk up to their stomachs the enlarged surface of their bodies and loads helped to stay their descent into the mud and sand. We were all up to the waist in water, obliged to take every precaution against being sucked down ourselves, while we had to disengage the animals which would all have perished without our help. First the loads were carried to the bank, each 100 lbs., requiring the efforts of six men, then the beasts were lifted out with levers of wood, and all were saved except two. This accident gave us six hours' hard work, and we encamped where we were, only a mile and a half from the town, since we could not pursue our march. We also had to dry all our wet things in the sun. We lost several curiosities in this manner, such as paintings and embroideries. Our food had not suffered at all, having been on the backs of the camels.

Our route from Moming to An-si-chou requires little description. The country which we crossed although forming part of the Gobi Desert from its shape, position, and climate, was not absolutely barren, owing to the presence of villages wherever there was a small stream, or a well to provide water, and foster the growth of a little grass. The track was not often trodden, to judge from its appearance, and when we had passed the small town of Re-ten-tze, the only travellers we met were an honest peasant, who was pursuing, at such speed as his donkey could compass, his daughter, who had eloped towards Hoa-rai-tse with a long-haired young gallant.

I would observe that the lakes marked on one of the maps of Asia published by the London Royal Geographical Society do not exist. A huge sandy basin is there instead, and no water is to be obtained in this neighbourhood, except from wells.

On the 19th of June we came in sight of An-si-chou, which, so far from being an important town, is a poor place half buried in the sand which the desert winds have heaped against its walls, and resembling Chen-fan in its position and its poverty. Once again we had been misinformed, and were to encounter the greatest difficulty in equipping ourselves suitably for what was unquestionably the hardest and most dangerous portion of our journey.

For various reasons we did not halt in the town itself, but having noticed good pasturages round the village of Pow Kankou, we pitched our tents on a threshing floor of earth stamped flat, sheltered by tall trees, which made an excellent camping ground. We were specially anxious to avoid the necessity of revealing our future plans in any way, and up to that time we had been able to keep our secret fairly well. We were afraid that the prefect of An-si-chou might suspect our intention of entering and crossing Tibet, and might oppose it, and still more afraid that he would attempt to assist us, and would encumber our movements with an escort of rascals. Accordingly, we thought it wise to have no dealings with this gentleman, and to achieve this, were obliged not to stay in his town. In An-si-chou we could not have refused to receive him; whereas at Pow Kankou etiquette would forbid him to visit us in our humble tent, and we could deal summarily with any envoys from him.

When travelling in China one must take a high line to avoid trouble; while in Tibet one must be unostentatious, and, above all, try not to attract attention.

On reaching the neighbourhood of An-si-chou I had given myself out as a humble merchant in search of furs and skins, who desired to enter upon the high tableland of Tibet to obtain them. I do not flatter myself that this story was believed by all whom we met, but I am sure that it never did us any harm, which is more than many explorers under their various disguises have been able to assert.

We set ourselves at once to hunt for the necessary provisions and animals. I say to hunt for; for a reasonable amount of stock could not be found in one place. One man could sell us 20 lbs. of rice, another 15. Under these circumstances it was hard to hunt up the thousands of pounds of rice, flour, millet, and peas which we needed for our maintenance. Transport animals were still more difficult to obtain, and for some days I really thought that we should find it impossible that year to procure pack animals, and to enter Tibet during the good season.

I had been impressed by the fact, stated in the reports of all travellers, that no sufficient nourishment could be found on the plateaux of Tibet for beasts, which died one after another, and thus imperilled the lives of the travellers who had ventured into these deserts. Accordingly, we had thought out a plan by which we hoped to reach our destination safely, even if we should find it impossible to get fresh victuals or to obtain fresh animals throughout our whole journey.

This plan, which was very simple, consisted in sacrificing the majority, about three-quarters, of the pack animals to the safety of the stronger ones, and not to attempt to bring any to our destination except those which were absolutely necessary. I reckoned that by loading thirty-five animals with peas for the nourishment of twelve others, when the grass failed or was poor in quality, and by abandoning these thirty-five when the provisions which they carried were consumed, I should about double our chances of success. I do not pretend to assert that this proceeding was wholly devoid of cruelty in itself, but I argued that it was far more inhuman and blameworthy to sacrifice the lives of my men to the safety of lower animals.

I had fully determined to take camels in preference to other means of transport, since they carried proportionately larger loads and ate less. But I had to give up this idea, for it was absolutely impossible to buy any of these animals. The few merchants at An-si-chou who possessed any had sent them out to pasture, and declined to send for them without receiving the full price before I could even see them.

Accordingly, we had to buy mules, and even asses, since there were not enough mules for our requirements. So we sent our people round all the villages in the neighbourhood, and in six days they managed to buy thirty-three pack animals. These, with the thirteen mules, four horses, and four camels already obtained on the way, raised the sum total of our baggage animals to fifty-four. Most of them were in good condition, and seemed able to bear the fatigues and privations of a journey across Tibet. We had certainly paid more than their value. Either the men had pocketed a round sum or the sellers had really forced up the prices. If, by chance, any other explorers undertake a similar journey, I strongly recommend them to buy all the animals they may need at Sining-fu or at Liang-chou—preferably at Sining-fu. It will not cost them more, and they will obtain animals used to mountains, precipices, snow, and even to glaciers—a combination of invaluable qualities.

The provisions also took six or seven days to collect, and were piled up in great heaps round our two tents, causing the greatest surprise to the peaceful inhabitants of Pow Kankou. We had overcome one of our last difficulties by obtaining camel's-hair bags which were quite new, and in which our provisions ran no risks of being scattered along the road, as had unluckily happened in January in the Gobi Desert. The men spent their time in making loads of equal weight, so as not to gall the backs of the animals, and in stuffing the pack-saddles which in China are always inadequately stuffed when bought. Our camp was a scene of great activity, especially when the animals returned from pasture in the evening, skipping and frisking in all directions, with no suspicion as to the sad fate which awaited them.

When the loads were ready, I had them weighed, and thus obtained an exact notion of the extent of our provisions. We had 6,000 lbs. of peas for the animals, 800 lbs. of rice, 700 lbs. of flour, 550 lbs. of millet, plenty of salt and sugar, and a little vinegar and Chinese wine. It was nothing much to boast about, nor could we expect much variety in our *menu*, but it was enough to keep us going, and I relied upon some lucky shoots to give us from time to time a good dish of meat.

It was only on the evening before our departure that the Mandarin in charge of An-si-chou decided to show any sign of life. He sent to me several of his subordinates in succession. I bowed them all out very politely, and assured them that the pleasure of shooting was quite enough to embolden us to face the privations and perils, of which they insisted on giving us a fearful description. As we were leaving Pow Kankou as early as possible the next day, I invited them cordially to visit me again in the afternoon if they wished for more details. Whether they returned or not is hardly a matter of history.

The 25th of June was a great day for us. We broke up our camp to move to the assault of the unknown plateau and the huge mountain chains which make Central Tibet practically impassable. I must admit that our first day's march was not encouraging. The animals, fresh after their stay of nearly ten days amid abundant pasturage, showed one after another an unpromising desire to throw off their loads and to return to the attractive neighbourhood of the deep grass. Some of them had the delicate considerateness to choose the moment of crossing a broad river for the execution of this intention, and thus threw the whole caravan into confusion. While our men worked up to the waist in water, at saving the sacks, my wife and I had the utmost difficulty in preventing the escape of the mules which had crossed first. The peaceful and unconcerned camels alone retained their dignity on this memorable day.

When we halted at nightfall we had covered but a very little distance, though we were almost tired out. Our ten caravan drivers pulled long faces at the prospect of other marches of this character, for the few miles that we had accomplished had in no way reduced the spirits of the beasts.

In fact the next day we advanced about 10 miles at the cost of much exhaustion, and, which was specially annoying, upon an excellent road, on which we ought to have been able to do double the distance without feeling it. To crown our troubles, we had no sooner halted and unloaded than half the animals thought fit to make a bolt towards the mountains. I spent half the night myself on foot among the outlying spurs, looking for my favourite horse, and only brought him back into camp after much trouble.

Nan Kankou, the point that we had reached that evening, is the last inhabited place on the great Gobi plateau, or, to put it differently, of the strip of land which here constitutes the furthest corner of Chinese Kansu. Directly south rise the first mountains, which, though small in height and cut off from one another by valleys running from east to west, unquestionably belong to the Tibetan system. Their appearance is wild and savage.

On the morning of 27th June, after a tiring night, due to the necessity of pursuing the escaped animals, which had fallen upon all, we had the pleasure of observing the rising of a hurricane of wind, sand, and dust. I will not dilate upon our troubles in marching under these conditions, but a few more days of this kind would have rendered further progress impossible. In the middle of the day we negotiated an easy pass, and after crossing the low range of mountains, found ourselves on the banks of a little river amid pasturage of astonishing excellence and extent. However, we did not halt, and pursuing our road towards a dip in the mountains some 20 miles away, we crossed a dry swamp, which, in the rainy season, must be quite impassable. After the swamp came a *saï*, a gentle slope, interrupted by ridges of sand, on which a little grass had taken root, and pitched our camp in a place in which no water or grass could be obtained. Our troubles had only begun; but at least our baggage animals had become more manageable.

In the morning the sky was clear, and the wind had dropped. The gorge to which I was leading the caravan was plainly visible, and we reached it after marching some 17 miles over firm ground rising about one and a half yards in a hundred, in a gentle and regular slope.

On reaching the mouth of this gorge we saw a charming and unexpected sight. A torrent of foaming water fell into a cañon some hundred feet deep, down a bed which it had dug for itself in the loess. Here and there the sharply-cut banks drew closer together. It could not be seen from the desert, in which it terminated, and even from a little distance it was imperceptible, buried as it was in its steep channel.

As we went on, we found that the gorge widened considerably, that the sides of the cañon sank to the level of the water, and that an oasis of grass and trees had developed in a well-watered corner, sheltered from the wind. We pitched our tent under some over-arching trees, beside the torrent, and let the animals loose to crop the grass.

An amusing incident occurred towards evening. Some honest peasants from An-si-chou, knowing the rich pasturage of this oasis, had taken up their abode for the summer in a sheltered spot a little to the south of that which we had selected, and were peacefully watching their herds of mules, asses, and sheep. When we arrived they took us for brigands, of whom there are plenty in the district, and having no idea of our numbers or of our real business, they bravely took up arms to defend their herds, which they supposed to be threatened. Thus it came to pass that as our men were beginning their preparations for a meal, we were aware of five men, armed with long Mongol rifles, who ordered us to decamp immediately. They had hardly issued this preposterous command when our people, relying on the superiority of our repeating rifles, threw themselves on the unfortunate herdsmen, disarmed them in a moment, and began to inflict a sound beating upon them. When I thought they had suffered enough, I intervened, and explained to them briefly wherein their mistake consisted, and how thoughtless actions bring unpleasantness to those guilty of them. Then I confiscated the weapons of these dangerous neighbours, promising to restore them when we started again next morning. A few minutes later they were on the best of terms with my men, and even sold us one of their finest sheep.

Our road next day, after following for some time the course of the torrent, traversed a wide desert plateau crossed by cañons dry at this season, which increased in number as we moved south. In the distance rose barren mountains, and the vegetation on the plateau itself was reduced to a minimum, consisting only of some bushes which the camels alone could eat. We had advanced in front of the caravan and disappeared from them for some time while crossing the dry ravines, and when at length we found a suitable camping ground on the banks of the river near which we had camped on the preceding evening, we found that we were alone. The caravan drivers, probably fast asleep on the backs of their animals, had lost our trail and wandered off. It was late in the evening when they rejoined us, exhausted by a trying march across this uneven ground cut by deep ravines.

During the last two days we had risen some 2,600 feet, and An-si-chou being about 3,800 feet high, we were now 6,400 feet above sea-level. It was the beginning of the great climb, and we only hoped we might never have to cross more difficult country. As long as we followed the course of the torrent marching was easy, and we avoided having to climb the surrounding ridges. The water was very low, and when we were compelled by a rock to cross the stream, the animals did not sink in further than the knees. Tamed by the work of the last few marches the pack-animals let themselves be led peacefully, and made no further attempts to get rid of their loads.

On 30th June we did not make a long march —only 8 miles. During the first days of our journey I thought it well to halt whenever we reached good pasturage, in view of the fact that we might afterwards have to do without it very often. We followed the gorge described, and approached a curious rampart of pointed mountains, at the foot of which the torrent suddenly turned to the right between two masses of rocks. A great number of torrent beds proved that the road we were taking must be almost entirely flooded and impassable in the rainy season, and at the melting of the snows. We found it quite easy and very picturesque. The water had cut its way across gravel, sand, and loess, forming here and there embankments of strange shape, fantastic arches, and grottoes of all kinds. Some camels must have passed over the road a few days before, for their footprints were still fresh.

On the next day we soon reached the end of the defile, and a broad, wide plain on a gentle slope spread before us, instead of the mountains which we had been threading for some days. We had crossed a second and more important chain which acts as a step towards the high ground of Tibet. At once I directed our course towards a dip in the mountain before us, and all day long we advanced in that direction over easy ground. In the evening we reached a slender stream which had been out of sight till then, just as we were beginning to despair of finding drinking water. It was perceptibly colder, which was not surprising, seeing that we had risen more than 3,000 feet on that day. We had covered at least 28 miles, and the animals showed signs of fatigue. The grass, too, was very poor, and would not be sufficient to support them for two days.

During the night a deluge of rain came down, and we had to cover our provision sacks hastily with felt and oil cloths. In spite of our precautions the downpour was so violent that more than a quarter of the sacks were soaked, and we had to dry their contents in the sun next morning before breaking up the camp.

We discovered some tents, inhabited by peaceful Mongols, in the small valleys across the principal chain. They were feeding their flocks of sheep, and could be seen riding about on all sides on their small ponies. They all wore fur cloaks, and so did we, for the wind blew with great violence, and the thermometer was near freezing point. It was useless to try and climb the rocky chain which rose before us, and I ordered a deviation to the right. After some 12 miles we reached a broad valley shaped like a rounded bay, in the middle of which we found fairly good grass. Accordingly we encamped, and received a visit from two Mongols, apparently small Mandarins, who informed us that our camping ground and a river which rose not far from our tents were called Ha She Ha. This place is apparently often visited, to judge from the remains of fires, and it must have some history, for, on a rock a little to the left before reaching it, are the ruins of a tower. This tower commands a magnificent view of the whole plain, and of the mountains which we crossed; and as the day was clear I took advantage of it to make an exact plan of the neighbourhood with the help of an eclimeter compass.

July 3rd was a very tiring day; we were continually crossing ravines from 30 to 120 feet deep, lying close together, and all running from south to north. Nothing was more fatiguing for the animals than this perpetual ascent and descent, which added considerably to the distance. The descent was sometimes so steep that the loads slipped over the heads of the beasts, and we lost much precious time in reloading them.

None the less, we rose 1,000 feet, and had still to cross two or three deeper ravines before reaching the end of the pass for which we were making.

Having once crossed this pass, and risen 600 feet more, we discovered a broad valley turning perceptibly to the north. As we saw no other road before us, and had no intention of climbing the steep rocky sides of the mountains, we went down the valley for some 15 miles. The bottom of the valley practically consisted of the dry bed of a great torrent, in the furrows of which many heads of *ovis ammon* were to be found. This fact alone would have proved how many of these animals inhabited the mountains to the south, even if we had seen none ourselves. There were also many skeletons of kyangs, or wild asses.

We came suddenly upon a Mongol camp

pitched at a place called Ta T'chuen, near copious springs and pasturages, which would have been very fine if the sheep had not cropped it as close as a carpet. We were hospitably received by ten Mongols wearing Tibetan dress, who sold us two sheep. They seemed much astonished at our presence, and could not understand why we had made so great a detour from our way to Zaidam, simply for the pleasure of fixing the site of certain mountains and valleys.

We spent the next two days climbing a succession of ridges and coming down into the deep valleys between them. It was very tiring work, and we made slow progress. Luckily there was plenty of grass. At the end of the second day we turned northward again, and having climbed a small height on the left bank of the river which we had been following all day along the well-marked tracks made by men and animals, we came upon the tents of a Mongol colony of some hundred souls, skilfully hidden in a small valley, which was furnished with a spring of pure water and rich in pasture. Flags flew on all sides, more especially near the dwelling of a petty Prince who came to meet us, and received us as well as he could in spite of his astonishment.

CHAPTER VIII

THE ZAIDAM MONGOLS

THIS Prince was the first chief of the great tribe of Zaidam Mongols that we had met, and the manner in which he treated us was enough to lead us to form a pleasant anticipation as to our future dealings with this tribe. He not only came himself to bring presents, chiefly of food, but when he heard that my wife was with me, he sent his consort and his daughters with gifts of welcome to her too. These ladies wore their hair streaming down the back, with imitation shells fixed to a piece of cloth which hung down behind.

The Prince made it his business to bring up and fatten camels which he sold at Sa-chou and An-si-chou, through a Chinese merchant who resided with him. He also sold boots, flour, peas, sugar, and tea at exorbitant prices to his own subjects. A pair of badly-tanned boots costs five sheep, and a pound of sugar two. The Prince seemed to have a special gift for trade, and possessed great wealth for a Mongol. He did not try to cheat us in our dealings with him, and he gave us a splendid camel in exchange for two of ours. These latter after twelve days' journey over the mountains were hardly able to move, and could not carry any load.

He gave us an old lama as a guide. This man was to lead us by the best road, first to the gold mines of local celebrity, and afterwards to the Prince of Zaidam, our friend's suzerain.

On the following day, under the guidance of the old lama, we said good-bye to this hospitable Prince. We did a good day's march to the south-west. Gaiety was provided by the record of falls from a horse obtained during the day by our cook Hoa. He, being a very bad rider, the caravan drivers had amused themselves by persuading him to get on a black pony which was very strong, but full of vice.

Hoa had consequently hooked on to his saddle all the utensils that he generally carried about with him, a teapot, tin cups, a water-bottle, and flour cakes, half baked, with which he now and again regaled himself. He had scarcely mounted when all this *bric-à-brac* began to clatter, the pony was startled by the noise, and departed at full gallop towards the plain to northward, having previously deposited his unfortunate rider in a convenient hole.

The Mongols brought the animal back late in the evening, all the utensils having disappeared, either lost or stolen. I thought it as well to confine Hoa's equestrian ambitions for the rest of the journey to the back of a stolid mule.

We marched in a south-westerly direction, across ravines caused by the torrents which came down from the great mountain chains. Nearly all were dry. All along we enjoyed a splendid view of the huge plain in which Sa-chou lay, commanding it as we did from a great height. From our camp we could trace the course of the Ara-cha-gol, winding away like a gigantic yellow serpent till it was lost amid the northern plains. We were directing our march towards its banks. At sunset the view was really striking and impressive.

Later, at nightfall, I made two unpleasant discoveries. First, that our tent had been pitched on a bed of wild garlic, which gave off a most poisonous smell, and next, that all the men of my caravan were complaining of some trouble, one had bad eyes, inflammation of the eyelids, I think another had cut his foot, a third had pain in his stomach, while Hoa was very sorry for himself, and was cursing his comrades, to whose machinations he attributed all his misfortunes. A small bird with an orange-coloured tail came and sang near the camp in the evening, and by degrees peace prevailed, and sleep overcame the caravan, including, of course, the watchman.

We reached the banks of the Ara-cha-gol or Tan-Ho on 9th July, after a good day's march. The ground had gradually become more level as the ravines subsided, so that we moved at a quick pace. I had directed our course since the morning so that we might reach a place specially marked on the Royal Geographical Society's map as being of some importance. It is called Gachun, and was in fact formerly the residence of a Mongol chief of the Zaidam tribe, but this half nomad has long since moved the seat of his small court to Tourainsien, not very far away, where purer water is to be had. Gachun is only represented to-day by some broken-down walls put up originally as shelters for cattle at night.

There are still on the banks of the noisy muddy river the relics of a fortified town, which must have been abandoned many years ago, to judge from the suggestion of walls and bastions which are the only trace of its former existence. This stronghold was called Tan-cheng, and is marked only on old Chinese maps.

We were surrounded by sheer desert. But for the sound of the noisy waters there would have been perfect silence. The Ara-cha-gol was pouring its yellow waters at a rate of 10 miles an hour over a rocky bed whose level was so irregular that rapids formed continually. The river was not very deep, not exceeding an average of 3½ feet, while its greatest breadth, when the rocks closed in upon it, was not more than 15 yards. But slight as this obstacle seemed it was yet too much for us to negotiate. The swiftness of the current, and, above all, the unevenness of the river bed, would have proved fatal to all our animals.

Accordingly, having spent a quiet night, we continued our march up the bank of the river. It proved a hard day. We had to make our way, following our old Mongol guide across dangerous defiles and steep passes, the mountains dropping sheer into the river bed. I wondered continually how the camels managed it at all, with their crushing loads on their backs, and their heavy clumsy feet often slipping on the stone heaps. We came down at last on the bank of the river once more, and as I did not want to go still further out of our proper course I decided to cross the stream at any risk, since the river at this point turned definitely to the south-east. I tried to get ropes fixed from one bank to the other, and with this intention I ordered Hia, our most active and capable man, to go into the river and attempt to reach the opposite bank. As a measure of precaution I tied a long and supple rope to him under the arms, and held one end of it myself, so that if he happened to be carried off his feet I could haul him quickly to the bank. It was just as well that I did this, for just as he reached the middle of the current, which was less swift as it widened out, he suddenly disappeared into a hole. We hastily dragged him towards us, and as the poor fellow, losing his head at his unexpected ducking, struggled and wriggled incessantly under water instead of assisting us, I had grave doubts as to a successful rescue.

This adventure having demonstrated the impossibility of fording the river at this spot we continued our march up the bank, and it was late in the evening when at last we found a place where there were four calm reaches. Here we crossed, and encamped on the left bank, on a patch of good grass.

As our caravan was composing itself to slumber, it was suddenly aroused by the barking of our little watch-dog Shishi, and we saw the dark and lofty shapes of some camels emerging from the gloom. Their drivers were as much astounded to find us encamped on the banks of the Tan-Ho as we were to see them arrive from the south. We were soon on friendly terms, and discovered that the caravan consisted of Sa-chou Chinamen, who were on their return from gold mines a hundred *lis* to the south, to which they had been carrying provisions.

I had not been aware of any gold mines further south, but was not surprised to hear of them, for the whole mountain chain that we were crossing, which reaches eventually to Ssu-chuen, is perhaps the richest mineral centre in existence.

Having satisfied my curiosity about the starting-point and nationality of these wayside acquaintances, I went back to my tent, while my men, greatly reassured by the sight of their fellow-countrymen, pressed them to share a supper consisting of flour cooked over a bivouac fire with the light of a tallow candle.

On 11th and 12th July we made a difficult journey over completely desert country along one of the small tributaries of the Ara-cha-gol.[1] We had to make our own road across the fragments of rock which occasionally so narrowed the valley as to compel us to tread in the icy water of the river or to cross it every five minutes. A march under such conditions was a sore trial both to man and beast. The animals varied very much in pace. The mules took only four hours to cover some 9 miles, while the asses took eight and the camels eleven. The latter were heavily handicapped by their long legs and their feet, except when it was a matter of jumping from rock to rock, or coming down almost perpendicular slopes. The landscape meanwhile was picturesque enough, but we were so tired out in the evening that all the beauties of Nature appealed to us in vain.

On reaching the spot at which our guide had assured us that there were gold mines we were at first disconcerted and disappointed. There were no buildings of any kind, and no traveller seemed at the time engaged in a search for the precious metal. However, having crossed the river for the last time, and settled the caravan, we set

[1] The Mongols call this tributary the Kakrousoun; the Chinese name of it is the Tincheko.

about finding the mines. They do in fact exist, in the form of circular holes, many of them not more than 10 feet deep and 3 or 4 in diameter. These holes have been dug in the deposits left by the river Kakrousoun, whose volume was formerly much greater, and which in those days detached part of their treasures from the semicircle of mountains which girdle its source. Some Chinese diggers come annually even now to wash out the alluvial deposits during the three or four months in which the country is habitable, greatly to the profit of the Mandarins to whom they are bound faithfully to hand over the results of their labours. The shape of the nuggets proves that they come from large deposits at no great distance. Some are large enough to suggest that they must have come from veins of great richness. No doubt a well-conducted working of the district would give excellent pecuniary returns.

Unluckily, such an exploitation is very difficult to accomplish, if not impossible, under present conditions. The climate would be the bold miner's first great enemy. Considering that a part of the river was frozen over on 12th July, it is not hard to calculate the severity of the cold in a winter. There is no pasturage in the neighbourhood; very occasionally some scanty grass appears in the grey-green patch. The wild yaks that visit this abandoned spot had long since eaten up the very little that had tried to grow there.

The Chinese Mandarins would also unquestionably view with disfavour a foreign exploitation, and if it proved successful would squeeze it to the extinction of all profit.

While examining the mines we came across three miners in a miserable hut hidden in a depression in the ground slightly sheltered from the icy wind. Our arrival at first affected them with an amazement almost amounting to terror, but a few kind words soon set them at their ease. Eventually they even showed us the gold they had found, with the very rudimentary instruments which they employ in washing out. They use for this purpose the icy water of the river, and no man can bear for very long the chill of its low temperature. They had only been at the mines for six weeks, and meant to return to Sa-chou-fu about the 15th of August. They had received one visit from a mule caravan which came to provision them, and to carry away their harvest of gold. They seemed quite indifferent to their very lonely and debasing manner of life, and thought it altogether natural to supply their Mandarins with gold nuggets in return for wages amounting to 8 *taels* per month.

We could not have stayed longer, for our beasts could not have obtained adequate nourishment anywhere, and it was most necessary to keep them in good condition.

I was therefore very reluctantly compelled to give orders to depart without having been able to make a thorough examination of the gold-bearing rocks.

On the morning of 13th of July the lama, who was to have guided us till we reached the encampment of the Prince Zaidam, suddenly disappeared. He had gone off to look for his horse, but he was not to be found at the time fixed for starting, and I left without him, being confident that I could advance quickly and safely enough with the aid of my sextant. The ground soon became, if possible, still more hilly and steep, and we tackled passes more than 1,600 feet higher than our camp that morning. Some sheets of unmelted snow and ice clung here and there to the bare sides of the mountains, and we were deprived of the magnificent view we should have enjoyed in bright sunlight by thick clouds which blocked the top of the pass. The summits on which we were moving commanded an enormous plain like a desert stretching out in the shape of an oblong basin, in strange contrast to the mountainous country which surrounds and protects it.

Leaving on our left a pass which seemed to lead too definitely to the south-east we began to descend a very steep slope, which was rendered more difficult by the loose stones upon it which were dislodged by the feet of the mules. After a few adventures and harmless collapses we reached a more gentle slope, where a slender stream starting from the mountains flowed towards the plain. The vast plain which now opened before us, and whose extent we were able to judge of, thanks to a lifting of the clouds, seemed hopelessly sterile. I therefore thought it as well to fill from the pure water of the little spring the water skins which provided for us and our men.

The ground became more and more sterile and dry as we went down. We were proceeding between mounds of reddish earth scooped out by erosion into fantastic shapes, and the grass became very scanty. Little by little the mountains round us lowered their crests, and at the end of our stage we could see behind us the lofty clefts of the chains we had just crossed, while we stood now on the natural border of the great plain.

We pitched our camp on a hillock of sand devoid of grass or water. The little stream had long since disappeared under the sand. We had to hobble our animals, to prevent their straying after pasturage and water, and to serve out to them a large quantity of peas. Some of them, moreover, were already beginning to show traces of fatigue, and their heavy loads had to be lightened.

At this camp we also made the acquaintance of the most impetuous and savage mosquitoes imaginable. Luckily they are not poisonous. Their existence requires some explanation, at so lofty an elevation, considering that the country is very dry, and that the winter cold must surely kill all the larvæ. Breschneider's German map, the only valuable one of Central Tibet, asserted the existence of some marshes in this vast plain. We did, in fact, in the morning see some dark green spots floating in a vivid mirage at a great distance.

I at once ordered the camp to be broken up and we moved as fast as possible towards these floating spots, hoping to find water. The way was easy, over a long slope of sand and small pebbles, with hardly perceptible undulations. The mosquitoes punished us cruelly, especially when we drew near to the marshes. The swarms hummed loudly, and rose in thick clouds around us. The marsh was partly overgrown with grass, and was caused by the stagnation of a small stream in its centre which flowed from the east. The noisome insects swarmed out of the grass and fastened on to the legs of our animals, which were soon black and bleeding. The poor beasts, distracted between their longing to benefit by the excellent pasture which lay spread before them and the acute pain caused them by the mosquitoes, made a gallant effort to snatch a meal, but were soon scattered in all directions, unable to endure the bites of their voracious foes. We had therefore to leave our tent half pitched, and to pursue the mules, which were galloping on all sides, maddened with pain and forgetting all their fatigue in their efforts to dislodge their enemies by rolling on the ground and tearing to and fro.

We suffered a good deal ourselves, for the meshes of our mosquito-net were large enough to admit a good many of the insects. Their ardour flagged for a while about midnight only. We then managed to get a little sleep, and the animals contrived to finish their meal.

All the travellers who have passed through Lolinor and the district twice traversed by Russian expeditions, in a slightly different direction to that taken by us, mention the great trouble they underwent from mosquitoes, and no such story is exaggerated in this respect.

On the bank of the marsh lay the remains of a Mongol. All his flesh had been eaten away, but the bones inside his clothes had kept some semblance of his original human shape. How had this poor fellow come to die amid such unkind surroundings? He was no doubt a diseased wretch, who had no beast on which to make his way back to his tent.

The next morning I decided on the unlucky experiment of crossing the marsh to gain time. At starting, the stretch of sand seemed solid enough to bear the weight of the caravan. But we soon reached a spot at which the dry and seemingly safe surface suddenly cracked and half swallowed our animals with their loads. It was as much as we could do to extricate ourselves from this false step, and we lost several hours through trying to gain one. We contrived, none the less, to cross the river at midday, and on reaching good ground again covered 20 miles before nightfall. We halted by the side of a small trickle of water.

On this march we met kyangs, or wild asses,

for the first time. They came about us in large troops to look at us and to frisk around. They would come up fearlessly within 50 yards of the caravan, and then suddenly bound away, kicking up their heels and biting one another. Sometimes they formed squares, or deployed in double lines, executing with elegant charm manœuvres and combined movements that might have been prescribed. Some of the troops contained two or three hundred animals, others barely twenty. Several young ones were frolicking beside their mothers. At this season they had found enough grass for some months past, and were plump and muscular.

A somewhat absurd incident now occurred, which gave us superabundant proof of the perpetual fear of Mongol or Tibetan bandits which dominated our caravan drivers. As the night drew on the men who were watching the animals at pasture a little way from the tents saw in a mirage at some distance some galloping shapes, and, with the aid of their imagination, believed they could distinguish guns, lances, and banners. In a panic they flew back to the camp at racing speed, and rushed into our tent. "Tajen, Tajen," they said to me, "we are attacked. All is over with us!" One of them even began to recite the prayers for the dead. Unmoved at this edifying spectacle, I told him to get up at once and fetch my telescope. As soon as I had focussed it I soon saw that the supposed bandits consisted of a large troop of kyangs pursued by some Mongol hunters. On great occasions the Mongols are rather keen on the flesh of the kyang, and the unusual manner in which they were hunting the beasts, instead of waiting patiently on the look-out for them, showed that some unforeseen necessity had arisen, and I concluded that we should probably soon meet the Prince of Zaidam, who must at that season be making his customary tour among his people, collecting taxes, appointing officers, and administering justice.

In fact, next day, after traversing a hilly region which was evidently well peopled, to judge from the flocks of sheep, the camels, and the horses which were feeding on all sides, on the grey-green soil abundantly watered by the little river, we were much astonished at coming in sight of a great variety of horsemen. Mandarins and lamas mingled the bright blue and yellow colours of their trappings in the plains, galloping after straying horses, while a busy group was erecting, on the banks of a small tributary stream, the white cloth tents with dark blue stripes which marked the presence of some chief, who could be no other than the Prince of Zaidam.

If we were surprised, they were still more so, on seeing a company of strangers suddenly appearing. But they showed no indiscreet haste, and gave us time to arrange our camp. From motives of prudence, we chose a raised spot on the top of a conical mound from which we could command the position, and easily resist any attack.

The Tibetan Mongols are very different to the mild and peaceful inhabitants of the plains of Mongolia, and very much disposed to robbery, and even murder.

After about an hour some Mandarins of the lowest rank made their appearance, and insolently demanded in the name of their Prince who we were, whither we were going, and how we had made our way into that district. I made answer that I was not accustomed to give replies to under-bred persons, and that if their Prince wished to make our acquaintance he might come and see us. As they insisted and demanded our passports to take away and show to their master, I declared that I would on no account surrender them, and that if he was so anxious to read them I would show them to him when he came.

Thereupon the ambassadors retired, and towards evening we saw a small mounted troop leave the tents and ride towards us. I immediately ordered a red felt carpet to be placed on the ground in front of my tent, and I invited this august visitor to take his seat upon it. He was a man of unpleasing appearance, dirty, and untrust-worthy. He was not dressed in silk, but wore over his garment a strip of leopard skin, the mark of his high position. His two sons were with him, one a grand lama, and the other the heir-apparent. I showed him my passports, which he could not read, and handed to his lama son, who read them aloud to the great edification of his father and all the suite. Finding nothing in these to object to they asked us many questions about our plans for the future, and as to where we might be going. The Prince had only one piece of advice to give us—not to go further south. "When," he said, "you have left the borders of Zaidam, where alone my power can protect you, I shudder to think of what will happen to you. The Naitchi Tibetans are cruel robbers, regular brigands. Don't go that way. What will the Tsungli Yamen at Pekin say if I let you continue your journey, and meet with misfortune? I shall be held responsible and punished."

This was the pith of the speech His Majesty deigned to favour us with, but when he saw that it produced no effect, he simply laughed and shrugged his shoulders, as if he washed his hands of the matter. He then began a close examination of our weapons, and was very greatly astonished at the distance of their range. If I had listened to his entreaties I should have absolutely wasted fifty cartridges, for, not content with firing a shot himself, he wanted all the Mandarins and soldiers of his escort to share this unique pleasure. He made me a generous offer of 51 *taels* for a Mannlicher rifle, and was much offended at my refusal.

At last, realising that he could get nothing out of us, and that we wanted nothing from him, he decided to return to his tents, and went off at a canter. He had hardly left us when a tremendous downpour broke out which lasted for twenty-four hours, and gave us plenty of food for reflection. The rainy season had begun. It lasts, as a rule, from the beginning of July to the beginning of October, and literally floods the Tibetan plateau. Where we were the inconvenience of it was less serious, since as the country is largely intersected with rivers and ravines, the water easily flows off. One cannot keep a dry stitch on one, but a caravan can advance without much extra difficulty.

At the Prince's request we stayed for one whole day near his tents. I had hoped to get a guide from him, but he declined, and his only reason for pressing us to remain was that he might renew his temptations with regard to the sale of arms. However, our stay was productive of one good result, for our guide, who had so disingenuously deserted us at the gold mines, reappeared; I easily persuaded him to accompany us as far as the edge of the Zaidam basin, but could not induce him to venture with us across the Salt Desert. "I am too old," he explained, "for such expeditions, and since you found your way so well by observing the stars, you will easily cross it without a guide."

On the 18th of July we resumed our march southward, making for some snow peaks which rose like a spiked gate at a height of 2,500 feet above us. As we approached them up a slight slope we saw about us the tracks of wild yaks, seemingly fresh, and, yielding to a love of sport, I let the caravan go on with precise orders as to its direction, and went in search of big game, taking with me Tschrung, the best shot among the men.

We climbed for hours up very steep summits, and, scaling the range I described above, we reached the upper snows without sighting anything. I was quite done up on my return to camp by this back-breaking stalk at a height of over 14,500 feet; and yet we were destined to rise more than 20,000 feet without feeling any evil effect from it, so great is the resisting power to be derived from habit.

For three days we traversed a country without any striking features, consisting of small chains of mountains, one after another, separating valleys which were often marshy and afforded in their depths good pasture, infested, unfortunately, by mosquitoes. The whole district was inhabited. Isolated tents here and there on the mountain sides, and collection of dwellings, wherever the comparative excellence of the verdure allowed of several families living together, proved this. The people were not engaging, and were very different from the Mongols in the Gobi, the latter being always ready to greet one. The inhabitants of these regions came out of their tents influenced solely by curiosity, and when we pitched our camp used to come and finger our sacks and boxes and try their weight with unparalleled effrontery. But for a vigilant watch many things would have disappeared. I had to get up two or three times every night to see that the watchmen were doing their duty, and though I often found them asleep, their own exceeding fear of the occupants of the neighbouring tents helped to keep them awake.

Although the rainy season had already set in we still had five days neither hot nor cold, and as we had gone down 3,000 feet from the level of the Prince of Zaidam's encampment, our journey was easy, and rendered still more agreeable by the practical certainty of finding a good camping ground each evening.

From time to time we ran across caravans of Chinese merchants. These adventurous traders came from Sining-fu to buy sheepskins at a low price, and to sell bad leather shoes, sugar, and dried raisins at ten times their value. These commodities are not sold under the most appetising conditions either. They are coated with dust and mixed with small pebbles to add to their weight, but once thoroughly cleaned they are excellent and last for ever. The last group of Chinese merchants that we met had with them a caravan of asses carrying more than a thousand sheepskins. These men were very young, and their manners were polite.

On the 21st of July, after crossing some wide grassy plains, the home of myriads of mosquitoes, we encamped near a Mongol village of twenty-five tents. This was the largest encampment we had met with, due to the special excellence and abundance of the herbage round about. The flocks born and reared in this district pay little heed to the mosquitoes, and, as the Mongols themselves are hardly worried by bites that would madden a European, all is for the best in this retired corner of the world. Its name is Ikra Zaidam, and it is the jewel of the principality.

It is one day's march only from this village to the Prince's palace. Having changed the south-easterly direction that we had been taking for two days to one more southerly, we crossed a ridge of bare hills running from south-east to north-west, and came out upon a great circular plain. This is enclosed round three-quarters of its circumference, has fat pasture land in the centre, and a blue lake glittering to the south. It is the Prince's special domain.

As soon as we reached the northern edge of the pasture we halted. The spot was a most suitable one for our camp. Water flowed close at hand, and we could see the royal tents not far away.

During the night, however, we met with an adventure which was not pleasant for tired people. Apparently the Prince takes in as paying guests horses and mules that are exhausted or wounded, at the charge of the Chinese merchants of Kansu. These animals recruit themselves for months in the luxurious pastures, and are there in great numbers, herds of several hundreds wandering about. In the course of the night one of the herds made advances to our caravan animals, and, having doubtless pronounced in glowing terms an eulogium on liberty, induced them to join in a wild stampede. Luckily our pack beasts were tired out by their recent marches, and could only play a very modified part in the stampede, owing to which good fortune we managed to get them back into camp after pursuing them for some hours.

Here also it was that we gave up for good and all paying the native in money. As towards evening we could not obtain a little milk or butter for less than one or two *taels*, a preposterous charge proportionately, and a "squeeze" that the most unscrupulous tradesmen in London or Paris could not rival, we decided to barter instead. So it came about that we got what we could not purchase for several shillings in exchange for two knitting needles. Intending travellers, please note.

After a calm and, as it seemed to us, very hot night, the thermometer standing at 18° cent. minimum, we set out again at an early hour. First we crossed the great grassy plain, waving under the wind, and came to the banks of the lake. This was beautifully blue and perfectly clear. Besides the herds of animals that I have spoken of, camels were to be seen on all sides, plump with the good cheer they had been feasting on for months. Hia, with characteristic Chinese patience, amused himself by counting them. According to him there were three thousand of them. Such wealth in cattle, added to his twenty tents and his two shops, makes the Prince of Zaidam the leading Mongol millionaire.

But an explorer does not attain all his desires on the shores of this exquisite blue lake. For although several little springs of drinkable water afford refreshment to man and beast on the northern side of the plain, it is not so to the south. Here the absolute lack of sweet water makes life impossible and camping difficult. It was only by digging a sort of well 5 feet deep that we could obtain some muddy water which we had to manage with. I was the more annoyed because our animals were about to undergo a severe test in crossing Zaidam, and I was anxious to give them abundant food and drink before entering upon it.

On the next day, after passing the low but bare ridge known as the Trsongin Ulan, which closes the basin of the lake to the south, we found ourselves confronted by the most desolate country conceivable. There are some views in nature that are more dreadful, there are some more terrifying, but none so disheartening. On the "sai," all down its infinitesimal slope, all traces of vegetation had entirely disappeared. There were not even those shrubs, half grass and half tree, which satisfy camels, nothing, absolutely nothing. In a shimmer of grey-blue, now looking like mirage, now like mere distance, the huge salt basin does not even suggest itself. It looks as if the slope you are treading must extend for ever. The desolation was as complete as in the most desert parts of Mongolia, but in addition there was the feeling that behind the fantastic glimmer of the mirage lurked hitherto untried perils.

We encamped by the side of a thin trickle of water that came from the Trsongin, but continued only for a few hundred feet in length.

CHAPTER IX

IN CENTRAL TIBET

THE crossing of the dry salt lake which forms the centre of the Zaidam depression, was most difficult, and I understand that it is not readily undertaken even with fresh animals. We started on the morning of 25th July, but under rather bad conditions, for, as I have said, our animals had not found good pasturage during the two preceding days, and the water that we had met with had been of worse than inferior quality. The men were expecting to encounter the most appalling disasters on the way, and they handled their driving whips without conviction. Evidently the great open space lying before us terrified them, and I was not entirely free from anxiety myself, for, according to the information I had gathered from the natives I had questioned at our recent camps, there lay on the other side of the great salt crust stretches of softer mud, into which a carelessly conducted caravan might easily sink.

My wife and I placed ourselves, therefore, at the head of the column, when, having accomplished the descent of the lake slope, which brought us to a level 600 feet lower than that which we had left, we reached the sand dunes immediately encircling the bed of the lake.

After crossing these dunes we came upon a slough of mud and salt water, which, however, it was easy to cross by moving from one hardened spot to another. On all sides holes yawned in the mud. It was impossible to determine their depth, but a sounding of 20 feet failed, in many cases, to reach the bottom. Some of the most treacherous of these swamps are covered by a thin surface of dry mud, which gives way at once under the lightest weight. It is none the less easy to discover them, owing to the fact that they are always slightly lower than the really hard ground. They are usually 1 or 2 feet across at the top, and never more than 3.

Having crossed the swamps we reached a stretch of dry mud with an even surface, on which the animals could proceed with perfect ease. After some time we came upon the tracks of a large flock of sheep, which had evidently crossed the lake but a short time before us, for the carcasses of the victims, left behind by the flock, were not yet decomposed. We were surprised to think that sheep should have accomplished this difficult crossing, which their slow habits must render still more dangerous, without any grass to sustain life, but the fact only proves once more what many explorers have maintained, namely, that of all the beasts capable of enduring the terrible hardships of life in Tibet the sheep offers the greatest resistance and endurance.

The discovery of these tracks proved very useful to us, for we decided to follow them, thereby removing all doubts as to our course, and avoiding all danger, as the animals, under the guidance of the Mongols as well as of their own instinct, had carefully avoided those places where the soft mud would have impeded their course.

We were congratulating ourselves on the ease of the journey hitherto so much dreaded, when we suddenly noticed a change in the surface of the dry mud, which was now covered with flakes of hard crisp salt, lying edgewise and like the blades of a knife in many places, so that our progress suddenly became extremely laborious. The camels' feet were soon bleeding, and the mules and donkeys followed their example, for the depth of their hoofs could not protect them when they slipped on the smooth surface of the salt. In a very short time the camels could hardly drag themselves along. The poor creatures were a pitiable sight. They peered with terror into this new ground, sniffed at it, and refused to proceed further across country which hurt them so cruelly.

Nevertheless, we were obliged to go on and reach the other side, so I gave the strictest orders that they were to be urged forward.

At nightfall the caravan was divided into two parts, and of course the animals had only a meagre supply of peas to eat. We had a little water, but only for the men. A cold, moonless night fell upon the improvised camp, where man and beast strove to find rest among the broken blades of salt.

At four o'clock next morning all were astir, for none had closed their eyes a moment, and we began to sweep the horizon in hope of discovering the rest of the caravan. I was apprehensive about it, for I reflected that if they had continued their journey during the night, in the hope of rejoining us, they must certainly have lost their way, as they had no landmark of any sort. Towards six o'clock, by the help of my field glasses I espied Hia and the camels following upon our tracks, and so soon as they had rejoined us and had, like the others, tried to appease their hunger with a little roasted millet, we continued our journey.

After a little while we noticed, on our right, a basin of pure salt which shone with dazzling whiteness. The Mongols have named it Doboson nor, and it may be called the keystone of the great dome of the Zaidam Lake. Its shape is irregular, and variable too, to judge by its borders. Its length and breadth would amount to 500 or 600 yards at most. Almost immediately after leaving Doboson nor we came upon the dry mud again, but this time without the blades of salt. But the mud was soon exchanged for a horrible mixture of earth, salt, and water, involving risk and danger to our progress, for it was impossible to avoid frequent falls into the quagmires among which we moved. Evidently this second part of the Zaidam Lake receives large quantities of water in the rainy season and when the snows melt. This opinion was still further confirmed when we reached river-beds hollowed out in the mud, and all sloping towards Doboson nor. They were dry at this season, for the spongy soil absorbed what small amount of water they might have held.

At length, after struggling through the mud for some hours, we caught sight of a row of tall reeds in front of us. We knew that water could not be far away and that we should now be able to let our beasts rest. However, we had still to cover several miles southwards before we came upon the water in little rivers, where we were able to pitch our tents on a favourable camping ground, to the great joy of the whole caravan. The name of the spot was Tassara, the rivers belong to a certain river and lake system which the Mongols call Tadjinar, whose waters flow towards the north, especially towards Doboson nor which the water only reaches at certain seasons of the year.

Thus we had crossed Zaidam in two days, and, on the whole, without very great difficulty. We had only had to leave two animals behind, and the others would recover after a thorough rest. According to my calculations we had covered a distance of some 50 miles between Trsongin and

Tassara, including certain zigzags in the course without either water or grass. Considering that the animals had hardly had anything to eat since they left the king of Zaidam's camp, I think their endurance was indeed admirable.

After a day's rest we were able to resume our journey southward, on a flat clay soil which could easily bear the weight of the whole caravan. Here and there we caught sight of troops of ponies feeding in perfect freedom far from the tents. This would tend to prove that the country is not so infested with robbers as it is reputed to be. Our shelter that evening was a tent inhabited only by two old women, but we could hardly snatch a moment's rest, on account of the millions of mosquitoes which attacked us all night in famished hordes. Even the animals could hardly bear their bites, and they had to be closely guarded to prevent their breaking away in all directions, maddened by the inflammation of the sting.

On July 29th we were on the march again, in the same direction as before, now skirting the banks of the river Tadjinar, now working away from it on the left. There was quite a considerable quantity of water in this river, considerable for that part of the country, about 2 feet in depth, by 20 or 25 in width. The effect of this precious stream is very evident in the vast green plains, capable of feeding many flocks and herds, which rejoice the eye and form a curious contrast to the desolate white and yellow of the salt desert only a few dozen miles to the north.

The number of tents was growing considerably, but the poverty seemed to increase with the population. We had not yet seen such abject poverty laid bare in the broad light of day, even among the Mongols of the North, who are ranked among the most wretchedly destitute races.

The Tadjinar people are as little hospitable as they are rich, and we could not persuade them to sell us a single morsel of meat, though we begged earnestly and eloquently for it. We were in sore need of it, not having tasted meat for three days, and such was our disappointment, that for the first time in the course of our journey, I decided to treat the caravan to a bullock without the preliminary of obtaining the owner's permission to dispose of his goods. Accordingly, a bullet from a carbine gave us an excellent dinner and a provision against famine, without exciting the opposition of the Mongols, which I had half expected. The proprietor uttered a cry, pretended to shed a few crocodile tears, and then retired with a smile upon his lips and an ingot of silver in his hand.

It is worthy of notice that the inhabitants of the Tadjinar district are not good customers for Russian manufactures. With the idea of reducing our expenditure I made an attempt to sell some materials brought into Mongolia by Buriat merchants, but my advances were energetically repulsed, and I was informed that Russian cotton materials are inferior in quality to Chinese products, which, indeed, is true.

This is in truth a curious country. The southern part of Zaidam is an almost exact reproduction of the north, as regards aridity and desolation. The fertile strip of the Tadjinar district alone breaks the desolate monotony of the desert. The mountains which we were now to attempt were rather higher than those from which we had come, but the difference in appearance went no further. The mountains which stretched indefinitely before us from east to west are called by some Tolai, by others Torai. As a matter of fact, they bear the generic name of the Naitchi Mountains.

This is the name of the country which stretches southwards from these lofty peaks. The Naitchi-gol flowing into the Tadjinar is an important factor in the river system of this oasis and issues from a mountain range opposite to which we had come through gorges described by the Mongols as extremely difficult to cross. Prejevalski and Rockhill alone had attempted to follow their course for a certain distance, and they had both turned to the right and reached the populous valley where there are two encampments, Naitchi and Missuto, at a height of about 14,000 feet. Our plan was to push on due south, following a tributary of the Naitchi, hitherto quite unexplored.

We had hardly entered the Naitchi Valley when our troubles began. Steep cliffs of loess rose on our right and left, the soil we trod was pure loess. There was no grass, not even roots for the animals, nor water, save in the river at the bottom of the ravine, and this river, which had cut its way deeply through a crumbling soil, was not always easy of access. To crown all we were beset by positive clouds of mosquitoes, and in spite of all precautions, such as blocking the tent door with a mosquito net, it was impossible to enjoy a moment's rest. While taking the usual evening observations my hands were simply devoured in the space of five minutes. Mosquitoes at this height! The reader cannot be more surprised than we were, nor had we ever seen any creatures more desperate in their sanguinary work than the mosquitoes of Naitchi.

The following day I noticed, for the first time, signs of disaffection among the caravan drivers. They had until then maintained perfect submission, or at least the appearance thereof, but, excited by stories of brigands, robbers, and cut throats, with which the Mongols had stored their minds, they suddenly changed their tone and assumed airs of mutiny. I first noticed it while on my usual rounds on the evening of 1st August.

I was able to hear the men's conversation by standing close to their tent, though outside the shaft of light from their fire. They were more or less agreed upon the following points: Firstly, that I must be out of my mind to come to such atrocious countries when I might be living comfortably at

Pekin; secondly, that the instruments I used for reconnoitring were nothing worth; and, finally, that their best plan would be to vanish during the night and let us go on alone if we were absolutely set upon an expedition which must come to a bad end. I decided that the moment for showing myself had come, and suddenly made my appearance, which disconcerted them not a little. I informed them that I had overheard their designs and should therefore take all necessary precautions; to begin with, I should have all the provisions brought to our tent.

I pointed out to them how mad it would be to attempt to retrace the journey we had made from Liang-chou without a European at their head. They would inevitably fall a prey to the rapacious Mongols, and would at length be frozen to death in the attempt to cross a snowy pass. On the contrary, if they would faithfully accompany us, they would earn such remuneration as would raise them to the rank of important people in their respective villages.

With the object of distracting their attention, and to teach them a salutary lesson, I made them work all night at mending the pack-saddles, and I myself was obliged to spend much time in superintendence, which I should have infinitely preferred to enjoy comfortably stretched upon my camp bed.

The next morning, even had we wished to do so, we could not have followed the Naitchi Valley for long. We should have been obliged to cross from the right to the left bank, and that at a point where the tributary we intended to follow joined the Naitchi, the speed and volume of water being such that we could not have accomplished a crossing.

We pushed on due south and entered a gorge, the appearance of which gave us but little encouragement. High cliffs, worn by the water's action into steep peaks and sharp angles, frequently forced us to descend to the level of the river, only to toil up again over steep, rocky, and dangerous slopes. This was most exhausting, and we were making very little headway, so, after ascertaining that the depth of the torrent was not more than 3 feet, I sent the whole caravan into the water, and men and beasts went up the rapid stream.

All went well for some few miles, and if our progress was slow it was at any rate sure, but unfortunately we came to a point where the walls of loess were so close together that one could scarcely see the sky between their rocky summits, and the torrent rapidly increased in depth and swiftness. Nevertheless, I led steadily on, struggling against the water with more or less success, until my mule missed its footing and dragged me back to join the rest of the caravan. Thus we were forced back to our climbing, the perpendicular aspect of the walls of rock being, as is frequently the case, much exaggerated by the steep height of the mountains above the level of the loess. It is surpassingly wonderful how the creatures managed it at all, even the mules, but especially the camels with their ridiculously long legs. It is no less wonderful that after a day of such terrific effort we should find a little grassy spot whereon to rest.

Our night's rest was in no way interrupted, and for the first and last time I dispensed with the watch, feeling quite sure that our best safeguard lay in the difficulty of access to our encampment.

On resuming our march on the morning of 2nd August our hopes rose somewhat at the prospect of the way before us. The surface of the loess, which the water had not touched, seemed to present a firmer and safer footing. But within a mile we were again disappointed, for we were suddenly confronted by a perpendicular wall, projecting from a mountain and falling sheer into the water 150 feet below us. I was a little disconcerted at this sight, especially as there seemed to be no other way. The rain which had fallen during the night had swelled the torrent, an effectual barrier even before the rain, so we were forced to face the crossing of this arête or give up the journey in this direction altogether.

We consequently undertook to make a sort of cliff path by means of our pickaxes, choosing a spot where there was already a kind of ledge in the rock. This work, which lasted several hours, was followed by another, no less toilsome, namely, the passing and carrying of all the baggage. Then came the critical moment when the animals had to be led over the path. They were pushed, held up, and hauled over with ropes, and we managed it pretty well on the whole, save for one camel which slipped over the edge and was left hanging over the abyss unable to find any foothold for its hind legs. After many and painful attempts we were able to haul it up again, but the poor creature's skin was badly torn, and we could make no use of it for some time.

We encamped, exhausted, immediately after this dangerous crossing, and that night Hia, one of the best drivers, fell over a precipice while attempting to recapture a camel which had strayed in the darkness.

The poor fellow was carried back to the tents, and I was glad to find that no bones were broken. Nevertheless, he lay in a state of coma for some time, for his head had struck against a stone in his fall.

On 3rd August we came out upon a wide valley lying parallel with Naitchi-gol Valley, which runs from east to west. We came into it about half-way down, and it stretched away in both directions, a vast and desolate waste of country. It lay about 600 feet higher than the Naitchi Valley and was more desolate, though a trained eye could distinguish patches of different colours in the very far distance, which were in all probability tracts of grass.

In spite of firm soil and a good foothold we

crawled along very slowly that day, both men and animals being completely exhausted.

However, as we slowly journeyed on eastwards, I was able to make a general plan of the valley, especially of the streams. They all, without exception, rise on the southern ridges and flow due north until their course is abruptly turned by the ridges on the northern side of the valley. There they combine and form a river, dashing down the defile through which we had come with so much difficulty.

Many of these streams flowed through deep layers of loess in which no vegetation was possible. In the very few spots where a little grass had struggled into life a few kyangs were peacefully grazing. Though it seemed a cruel and all too easy sport to kill these graceful creatures, I decided to victimise one of them, with the object of giving some meat to the men and of economising our store of rice and flour.

At a distance of about 27 miles from the spot at which we had entered the valley we came to a ridge, which divides the streams into two different water systems.

The rivers still flow from south to north, but, instead of turning off eastwards at right angles, they flow towards the west, and on the evening of 4th August we encamped opposite to a gorge very like that which had brought us into the valley, though seemingly easier of access, and evidently leading into the Naitchi Valley.

The next day was somewhat sensational, for we encountered a herd of wild yaks for the first time.

The first detachment came out right in front of us as we were peacefully making our way southwards up a little stream, and we had barely time to hide the caravan behind some rising ground. We were not anxious for this meeting, for yaks have a reputation for attacking camels and baggage mules.

These superb creatures were really a grand sight, as they passed quietly before us, in number about two hundred, calm and majestic, sweeping the sand with their long black hair, with something both of strength and pride in their bearing. They took about half an hour to file past us, and when they had almost disappeared behind the southern chain I could not resist the temptation of a shot, and fired on the last of the herd. I hit him full in the chest, but not in a vital spot; he did not fall, but, catching sight of us, came galloping towards us, lashing his bushy black tail. A gully in the loess checked his course for a moment, and I lodged another bullet between his eyes, which killed him instantaneously.

He was an immense creature. The thickness of the neck was perhaps the most remarkable point about him, the tough hide bore the marks of many blows from the horns of the other males in the herd.

We cut off some of the meat and resumed

our march. But we had not yet finished with the yaks, for a few miles further on, in an absolutely exposed part of the country, we suddenly saw three enormous bulls charging towards us with all the speed of their powerful, heavy gallop. I had often read in books of travel that a yak, if not mortally wounded, will sometimes charge its enemy furiously and with lowered head. But in this case the terrible creatures were attacking us even before we had seen them, and our position was critical indeed. As I have said, there was no sheltering ridge to be seen, and we shuddered to think of the awful havoc the yaks would work among the heavily laden mules and the camels. Our only chance was to stop the brutes as soon as they should come within easy range. So I dismounted, and, as our one chance of safety, brought up my Mannlicher. When the shot was fired, to my great relief I saw the leader fall on his knees and roll heavily over at 300 yards from us. I was about to fire on the two survivors when I saw them stop, sniff round the body of their dead comrade, and, turning back in the direction from which they had come, flee with all speed from the spot.

We soon found that the animal just killed was still huger than the yak shot in the morning. The bullet had caught him just between the eyes. We only cut off his tail as a trophy, and left him to the vultures of the desert.

By pushing steadily on we had reached what

NOMADS OF TIBET AND THE TENT MADE OF THE HAIR OF THE YAK.

[*To face p.* 216.

I may call a second story in this remarkable valley. We had climbed about 1,500 feet in one day, almost without noticing the rise, so easy was the gradient. We did not wish to continue the journey eastwards, for it would have led us too far away from our course, besides covering the track of other explorers; so we decided to bend to the south by a snow-covered pass, crossing the source of a glacier.

Though not in itself very alarming, this pass proved too much for two of the caravan men, who were unable to keep up with us, though they were both riding mules. We were thus obliged to encamp in a place without a blade of grass or a drop of water, for fear of losing these two men altogether. This was the more likely, as a strong wind was blowing, which would soon have covered the faint track which the caravan might have made in its passage over a hard soil.

Grass! grass, and rest! It was a crying need. Grass for the exhausted mules, and rest for the hard-worked men. But the question was where to find grass. All around us was a brown and sterile soil; as far as the eye could reach the great undulating waste was barren and inhospitable. We were beginning to despair when, on the morning of 7th August, as I was anxiously scanning the horizon through my field-glasses, I saw several herds of antelopes all making for a little dip on the southern mountain line a few miles away. This gave me the clue for which we yearned; the fact of so many animals all making for the same place pointed to there being water and pasturage to be found there.

We set out forthwith, but found we had to face a rocky climb of 900 feet before we could gain the pass, though it seemed but a mere dip in the chain when viewed from below. But we were repaid for our trouble by the superb view we now had of the mountains we had crossed the day before, on the southern side of the huge valley. The snowy peaks stood out dazzlingly bright in the sunshine, and several of them now gave an impression of much greater height than we had at first attributed to them. There was something grand and stupendous in the very desolation of the scene. We gazed upon it for a long time, in rapt admiration, yet there were still greater splendours awaiting us in the south.

We had been right in our judgment; for the descent from the pass brought us into a gently sloping valley, the sides of which were covered with grass. Judging from the enormous number of bones which lay strewn about, bones of yak, antelope, and *ovis ammon*, it was the *rendezvous* of all the dwellers in that desolate land, who evidently came there to find pasture when there was none elsewhere, often dying there from the hardships they had undergone. Considering what the winter must be at a level of 15,000 feet it is astonishing that any life survives.

It was an oasis indeed for people who had

seen no grass, nor even a semblance of green, for days. The pack mules did not even wait to be relieved of their burdens before they started grazing.

It was high time that they should find some nourishing food. We could not give them enough peas to make up for the want of grass, and five of these strong creatures were already stretched stark and stiff upon the road behind us.

We now gave ourselves up to the sheer delight of a thorough rest. I gave orders that the tents should be put up for a two days' halt among the pastures. Yaks and antelopes galloped past on every side, and kyangs, full of curiosity, came to graze with our mules.

It was this very curiosity, I may say familiarity, on the part of these kyangs, or wild asses, which brought about the disappearance and subsequent loss of two of our best mules. I had given strict orders that the mules should be fettered to prevent any chance of escape, but the men, who were convinced that the creatures were too weary to dream of escaping, neglected my orders, and allowed them to graze at large.

It was doubtless during the night that a company of kyangs came among our animals, and I suppose it was the sight of these fiery creatures in the joy of their liberty which decided two of our mules to join them in their life of risk and adventure.

I was obliged to send some of the caravan

drivers in pursuit of the wanderers, and thus the punishment of working during a whole day of rest came upon the very men who had been guilty of such unpardonable negligence and disobedience. But this was not the end of the adventure. I had hoped to see the men back by midday, or, at the latest, by sundown, but I was to be disappointed. As they had not returned by ten o'clock at night I decided to go out in search of them. My mule saddled, I wrapped a thick cloak round me and set out, with our faithful dog Shishi, whose keen scent had more than once been requisitioned for the caravan. But I had hardly started when a fearful storm broke over us, a storm of such hail and snow that every vestige of a trace was obliterated, and search would have been futile. So I returned to the tents as best I could to await the following morning.

Next day, to our great relief, we could distinguish two dark figures coming towards us across the white fields of freshly-fallen snow. They were the two lost men, who had seen the camp from afar, and were trying to rejoin us. The mules were lost for good and all. We were able to trace their shoe prints for about ten miles, intermixed with the tracks of the kyangs, but then they were lost upon a hard surface which had retained no impression. It was useless to make any further attempts. The only wise course was to push on.

From our comfortable camp we left the valley by an easy descent and reached the wide plain which lay to the south. From there we could see that the valley we had just left was only one among many others of the same shape. But while the others were barren ours was watered by a little stream which never ran dry.

As we advanced we began to realise the nature of the plain and its dangers. On all sides of us were bogs, pools of water, and stretches of grass. For two or three hundred yards one could walk safely on firm soil, then suddenly one's feet would sink into soft, deep mud, out of which it was most difficult to struggle.

There were rivers flowing here and there, which would lose themselves in the sand and suddenly reappear a little way off. This indicated the presence of many streams, some with a visible course, and others subterranean.

There was no lack of game, from the little straight-horned antelope to the largest yak. But there was no trace of human habitation, no vestige even of human existence. This was a region quite off the beaten caravan track, and the abundance of game proved that the foot of man never trod this inhospitable soil.

We spent several days crossing this great plain, travelling first south-south-west, then west by south. An abundance of water, of grass, and of game rejoiced our hearts, and we should have been quite happy had it not been for the quagmires from which we could not altogether escape. Some of them were so extraordinarily concealed that the most experienced eye could not detect them. They occasioned many a fall and indescribable confusion, especially when we had to cross two rivers, presumably tributaries of the Yang-tse-kiang, judging by the direction in which they were flowing. Wellby, the English explorer, often camped upon the banks of the second of these rivers, when he was crossing North Tibet, between Kashmir and China.

The lake scenery here was often very charming. Grassy dunes framed the sheets of water, and numbers of wild duck rested on the still surface. Of these we made a regular massacre, for a wild duck cooked in its own gravy, served with rice and fried potatoes, is the Tibetan equivalent for a dainty supper at Paillard's! Unfortunately, these sumptuous feasts are of rare occurrence, and the *menu* consists, as a rule, of boiled rice, potatoes, millet, and occasionally a slice of grilled yak. When it was very cold we used to take a glass of Chinese wine to warm us, and, personally, we have never experienced the ill-effects which certain explorers attribute to brandy taken at high altitudes.

I recollect how one day, when I was on in front of the caravan, I suddenly came upon a grassy place, behind a sheltering bank of sand dunes, where two great yaks were peacefully feeding. The nearer of the two was but 30 yards away, and I quickly shouldered my rifle without even dismounting. The bullet hit the spine of

THE SOURCE OF THE YANG-TSE-KIANG.

[*To face p.* 252.

the first animal, and the second fled away. Approaching then with my revolver I fired at the beast's head, at which it merely shook its mane. It was wounded in six places before it expired: surely a proof of extraordinary vitality.

This journey of a few days' duration across an almost level country was one of the pleasantest parts of the expedition. But, unfortunately, it did not last long, and we were to face fresh difficulties only a few days later.

On 12th August we left a defile in which we had found plenty of grass, growing indeed 2 feet high in some parts, though of an extremely coarse fibre. We emerged, by a pass 900 feet above the plain we had just left, upon a plateau where a curious effect was produced by the heaps of sand which stood out in sharp contrast against the darker soil beneath.

We crossed this new plateau in three days, covering a distance of about 50 miles in a south-south-westerly direction. We were occasionally on good soil, but much oftener on quicksand or horrible bogs. The last day was the worst, and we were obliged to desert a camel which had sunk in so deeply that we could not save it, especially as it manifested a complete and obstinate inertia in the whole matter. We crossed many streams, all flowing towards the south-east, and the reader has by this time realised what is involved in the crossing of a Tibetan river with a mud bed. All the baggage has to be carried across, the men helping the animals. It is killing work, and in this case it was aggravated by torrents of rain which had poured upon the caravan unceasingly for days, varied only by occasional showers of hail.

One difference between this plateau and that which we had crossed three days before was the practically total want of game. This phenomenon, at first inexplicable considering the abundance of grass and water, ceased to puzzle us when on the 13th of August, in the evening, we found that we were reaching the obviously beaten track of the pilgrim caravans that pass to and fro between Lhasa and Sining-fu. Our suspicions were confirmed by remains of bivouacs, bits of cloth, an occasional old boot, and carcasses of horses and donkeys. One caravan must have passed quite lately, for the traces of its fires were still fresh.

The mountains which close in this plateau are pronouncedly red in colour and very much cut up by many valleys, each of them the source of a small river. They are called Dungbura, and run from east to west, or rather to south-west. We struck them at about 34° 35′. They are well known, and have a high repute among Chinese and Mongol pilgrims for the excellence of their vegetation. Prejevalski crossed them in 1873, but much to the west of our route.

Here again we had to give the exhausted caravan a day's rest. The men were beginning to show unmistakable signs of fatigue. When a Chinaman throws himself on the ground and refuses to eat at the end of a march it means that he is fairly well tired out. We were sorry for the poor fellows, but could do nothing to assist them. Our only hope lay in pressing forward rapidly. We could only trust that the Tibetans of Lhasa and Shigatse would not block the way. If they did, very few of us would reach Kashmir, which would be our only alternative course.

Besides, my wife's plucky example might well encourage them. She often shared my watch at night, and although by day she helped right and left she was still full of energy.

On one day of rest on the northern slopes of the Dungbura Mountains the sun was kind, and we were able to dry the clothes and blankets which had been completely and continuously soaked during the previous week. We started again on 15th August at 6 A.M. The beasts set off at a good pace after their rest, but, unfortunately, did not keep it up long. We had to cross a lofty ridge whose summit consisted apparently of mud, then to go round through defiles, climb steep points, struggle across swamps, and scale more muddy uplands, to reach at length another wide plain closed to the south by mountain chains similar to the one we had just negotiated.

The whole country seemed of the same pattern. A series of wide plains separated by mountains running in the same direction, each plain, as we moved southward, slightly more elevated than its predecessor. It was very monotonous.

We continued to follow the caravan road. We intended to leave it later, but, so far, we had seen no pilgrim caravan on the march, and we did not want to miss the sight.

All along the road inscriptions in honour of Buddha were cut upon poor stones or upon projecting rocks. The fanatical superstition that has caused stupid Mongols and Tibetans to set up these monuments is not unique. Is it not to be witnessed every day in some parts of Europe? There it has less excuse, since those who practise it live in the full sunshine of modern culture and civilisation.

16th August was a great day for our little expedition, for we saw some human beings for the first time since we had left Zaidam and its Mongols.

We had scarcely begun our march, at about 8 A.M., when we suddenly perceived some riders cantering along over the sand of the great plain, carrying long sticks decked with flags of various colours.

They rode up to meet us, and alighted.

CHAPTER X

ALONG THE YANG-TSE-KIANG

We thought at first that they meant to stop us, or at least to ply us with questions; but this was not their object. Having scarcely looked at us, they proceeded to set up their flags in different spots, and to unsaddle their horses.

They were evidently only the scouts of a larger body; their advance guard soon appeared. It consisted of about fifty men, practically all armed, and riding small Tibetan ponies like those in the neighbourhood of Sining-fu. Some hundred yards behind them came a second corps, containing persons of evidently greater importance, for they were not armed, and the majority sat haughtily on caparisoned mules. Great herds of tame yaks followed, loaded with provisions, and driven by ragged men. A small troop of armed men closed this imposing procession.

We counted two hundred and twenty men altogether, rich merchants, lamas in red and yellow robes, soldiers, and yak drivers. About sixty were armed with rifles of Chinese manufacture, and some ten carried carbines slung across them, which seemed to me to be either Mausers or Winchesters of an old-fashioned type. In the eyes of their fortunate possessors such weapons are of inestimable value. They often fail to procure the special cartridges necessary for these arms; but the very possession of a foreign-made rifle gives its owner an assured position of respectability and impunity. One fellow in particular caught my eye. He wore, under the usual red Chinese button, a regulation forage cap which must have belonged to some English soldier who fell in the Tibetan Expedition. The sight of this trophy set us thinking. We had heard hardly anything of this little war, and I wondered for a moment what reception was awaiting us in the south, and whether our arrival might not excite a desire for vengeance to which we should fall easy victims.

All the members of this caravan, however, seemed well disposed towards us. As we passed them many of them greeted us with the words "rao ma," which mean "good horse"—a formula which is the customary compliment interchanged by those who meet by chance in the desert.

The passing of this large caravan lasted nearly an hour—a stream of life amid the surrounding sterility. We were far from the scouts and their flags when we saluted the rear guard, and when all had disappeared behind a hillock, the desert looked lonelier than ever, and the sense of isolation weighed the more upon us from having been momentarily dissipated by the passing of this great company of pilgrims.

For they are true pilgrims, these men who go to Lhasa in faith and piety, through all the many dangers that beset them in such regions. They face the cold, the brigands, and the heights that prove fatal to many. Mingled among the devout are some practical people and merchants, whose desire to receive the Dalai Lama's blessing is accompanied by the desire of filling their pockets. This year, however, they had to do without the holy man's benediction, for he had fled at full speed northward from the khaki-clad soldiers of England, to seek shelter among his Russian friends, who were also being hardly dealt with by the Fates. For some time it was not known for certain to which point on the Russian frontier the head of the Tibetan hierarchy had guided his mule. A Zaidam Mongol told us as we came through that country that the Dalai Lama had crossed the Naitchi a little to the west of the point at which we succeeded in crossing it, and that he was proceeding by forced marches to Uliassutai, with only three attendants, levying food and transport from the scanty population on his way. These poor folk thought themselves well repaid for the loss of their beasts by being permitted to gaze for a few moments on the features of one who is God to them. From Uliassutai he was going on to Urga.

As we rode slowly on along the track marked

by the pilgrims, I could not help reflecting on the manner in which history repeats itself. Etiquette changes and morals vary, but religions flourish everywhere. They all attain the same result. A small class of the self-styled elect is maintained by the credulity of the general public. As elect, they claim the right to distribute at will the precious blessing of heaven. All pilgrimages, whether to Lhasa, Mecca, the great Chinese temples, the African mosques, or the churches of Rome, spring from the same fundamental principles, and produce the same golden results.

After this eventful day we found the next specially monotonous, the more so by reason of rain, which fell unceasingly throughout it. This was the beginning of the real rainy season, very like that of India during the monsoon, the only difference being that the monsoon bursts about three weeks later in Tibet, and that more rain falls.

We encamped that evening on the banks of the Ulan-muren, a large tributary of the Yang-tse-kiang. Judging from its width, I thought the crossing bade fair to be very difficult, and, as I sat up for an hour's vigil, I did not look forward to it. The river ran silent and mighty, swollen by the rain, and occasionally sweeping down a portion of the banks with its resistless waters. I shall never really understand how we crossed it. Never during our whole journey was our little caravan so nearly lost. And yet on 19th August we were all safe and sound on the other bank, having only lost a few of our beasts.

We began the crossing on the 18th, early in the morning. I rode the strongest mule we had, and ventured into the water to try to find the shallowest ford. The river was divided at this point into eight streams, separated from one another by what appeared to be small islands of pebbles and loess, and I hoped to rest my beast on each island. But I had hardly reached the middle of the first stream, when my mule lost its footing, and began to swim valiantly. We went down stream about two hundred yards before its hoofs touched ground again, and I did my best to guide it to what I believed to be a safe landing. To my despair and terror, it had scarcely set foot on the first island when it sank up to its middle. It was a quicksand! I realised at once that if I stayed in the saddle I was lost, and helped by the instinct of self-preservation, I threw myself off and rolled on to the sand-bank. I felt it give way under me; but by lying on my back and opening my fur cloak I extended myself sufficiently to prevent being sucked into this fearful abyss.

Instead of trying to escape at once, I took some minutes to consider the situation, for the slightest wrong movement would have been fatal. I saw my mule, poor beast, disappear inch by inch, and in less than three minutes the sand had closed again over the tips of its long ears. This sight aided my decision, and I made up my mind to roll sideways towards the river, which was only 3 or 4 yards distant. Little by little I executed this manœuvre, and reached the water. Once there my task was simple; I threw off my fur cloak and swam. The water was so cold that I could hardly breathe or strike out, but at length I reached the shore, and soon afterwards the camp, from which my wife had been following the various steps of my adventurous career with great anxiety. It was madness, therefore, to attempt a crossing here, but it was not easy to find a better spot. For some furlongs both up and down the river seemed the same—streams of water intercepted by sand-banks.

Suddenly a ray of hope dawned on us. In the distance a troop of wild yaks were preparing to cross the river, and where these huge and heavy animals could pass we could, no doubt, follow. When I had seen them manage it safely I ordered the camp to be struck at once, and the whole caravan made for the point which seemed to promise an easy crossing. The yaks' instinct had led them right, for where they crossed the waters of the Ulan-muren were narrower, and enclosed between banks of earth and gravel, not of shifting sand. Unfortunately, the current was swifter and the water deeper. Only the camels could keep their heads above the level, and so all the baggage had to be sent over on them, while the horses and mules swam over as best they could. We set to work hard, and, the rain having ceased, the start of our operations was easier than I had dared to hope.

We were congratulating ourselves on our success when a fearful storm burst suddenly with oceans of rain. I have never seen heavier rain, and we soon noticed that the water-level was rising, and the current becoming perceptibly swifter. The camels could hardly keep their balance, and the mules were carried down some 5 furlongs before reaching the opposite bank. However, as there was very little baggage left to transport, we decided to get it all across before night. It was an unlucky decision, for, owing to a sudden swirl in the current, the last camel, which was carrying 400 lbs. of rice, lost its footing, and was swept away with its valuable load. This was a great loss; we might have lived for several days on 400 lbs. of rice, and our other provisions were nearly finished, thanks to the voracious appetites of the men. Moreover, that was not our only loss during this lugubrious crossing of the Ulan murcn. Three mules which had been carelessly left behind brousing peacefully, when they saw the caravan on the other bank, tried to cross by themselves. All were carried away beyond reach of help by the waters, which had now grown angry, and were much swollen.

For four days we continued our march across country composed of small hollows and bluffs of friable rock.

We reached the Yang-tse-kiang the day after crossing the Ulan-muren. This huge river was, when we struck it, restricted to a narrow bed, and the water was evidently deep. It flowed over gravel, and the high-water mark, many yards above its level then, showed what its depth would be after the melting of the snows.

Pastorage was richer and more frequent here. Large herds of wild yaks evidently came to feed on it, and I was lucky enough to kill one of them, which afforded juicy beefsteaks for all. We had had no meat for five days, and Europeans cannot live contentedly on rice and millet, however such food may suit the Chinese.

Occasionally we had to cross little tributaries of the Yang-tse, but they offered no difficulty, the only inconvenience attaching to them being the ice baths they made us take. During these few days of quiet travelling, we observed that many of my men found it hard to drag themselves along. Lao Chang, a Liang-chou man, seemed the most afflicted. He appeared to be overcome with a somnolence, which he could not shake off. At night he threw himself on the ground, and never stirred till next morning. He could not be relied on to watch the beasts, but as he still had an excellent appetite, we did not know what to make of him.

The moral condition of the men was also far from satisfactory. The grumbling and discontent of early days had been replaced by a kind of

THE DANGLA RANGE.

[To face p. 264.

hopelessness much more disquieting and difficult to deal with. Their easily depressed imaginations had been powerfully affected by the sight of the snow mountains in endless range behind the long plains, and by living in a country where no human being had apparently ever penetrated. Encountering a large caravan armed with rifles and yet apparently afraid of brigands, had done nothing to raise their spirits, and we began to have great difficulty in ruling our little army.

On 23rd August we could see in front of us the white peaks of the Dangla Mountains. To the south they seemed to set up a barrier difficult to traverse, which yet had to be overcome if we wished to follow the Yang-tse to its source.

The aspect of the country had changed. We had to keep close to the river to avoid the rocky spurs which ran out from overhanging bluffs, and our march became more difficult. The river had evidently forced its way through narrow gorges, and we doubted much whether we should be able to go far under these conditions. Towards evening a huge perpendicular cliff came straight down to the water in front of us, and we had to make a circuit which took us three hours, and led to an interesting *rencontre*. As we went down again towards the Yang-tse, along a narrow and precipitous little valley, behind a mass of fallen rock, we came upon an encampment of Tibetan hunters of the wild yak.

We were much surprised to see them, clothed

in their sheepskins; but our surprise was nothing to theirs. They gazed at us for some minutes, and then one by one began to escape towards the neighbouring heights. They were evidently very much afraid of us, and our magazine rifles, which they thought boded certain death, did not help to restore their confidence. However, we managed to catch one of them, and by fair words and the gift of a few pieces of sugar, of which Tibetans are very fond, we convinced him that our intentions were peaceable. Then he collected the scattered members of his family, and did the honours of his dwelling. I hardly know how to describe it. It was not a hut or a cabin, but a heap of rags in the shape of a tent, open to wind, rain, and inspection from without. We never saw a more miserable concern.

In a space of about 10 square feet, a family of eight enjoyed the sweets of existence together. Their dress suited their environment. Shreds of sheepskin partially covered them, and the cold wind blew on their bare skins without appearing to inconvenience them. The women looked still more wretched than the men; they were as nearly bestial as human beings can be.

Their method of life hardly tends to civilise them. They spend their time hunting wild yaks with guns of a primitive type, like the old match-locks preserved in museums, and, when they have succeeded in bringing down their quarry, they quarter it and cut the flesh into strips to make the dried meat which they sell in the winter at Lhasa or Shigatse. With the few *taels* they get in this way they buy a little more powder, and go off on a fresh expedition into the most desolate regions of Tibet.

These half savage hunters, and the brigands who are always lying in wait for the caravans, are the only people who live for a few consecutive months in the zone of the high central plateau. They are seldom met with, for they conceal themselves carefully.

Having spent a quiet night close to the yak hunters, we went along the Yang-tse with more hope and perseverance than success. In fact, we had hardly covered 2 miles before the road became absolutely impassable for the mules and camels. The rocks descended precipitously into the strong stream, and our only chance of progress lay in climbing the promontories, 500 or 600 feet in height, which blocked the way. In spite of the fatigue caused by this, we had decided to go on till we were stopped by some really insuperable natural obstacle. We came upon one before very long. One promontory which we tried to surmount ended in a rocky *arète* about 100 feet high, which nothing but an *ovis ammon* could have negotiated. We were therefore compelled to turn off into a valley which left the river at an angle of 50° to the west, and seemed to debouch into a wide plain in the direction of the Dangla Mountains.

This valley and its continuation nearly proved to be the termination of our journey, and the grave of the caravan. During the three days that we spent in it, we suffered more and worked harder than in all the rest of our crossing of Tibet. Here we fell in with the worst enemy—the irrisistible, clinging, ubiquitous, invidious enemy—mud!

My readers probably can form no idea of what mud in Tibet means, accustomed as they are to the annoyance caused by a few inches of it, for which they objurgate some negligent municipality. In Tibet, after a thaw, in some valleys and hollows which have no outlet, the mud extends for several miles at a stretch, and is occasionally so deep that it cannot be fathomed. Animals disappear in it as if in a quicksand, though more slowly, and when one realises that throughout a whole day's march one does not come across one square foot of ground which will bear one's weight, one can understand that a day's journey under such conditions is fearfully trying, and that the nights are even worse.

For three days we had to struggle incessantly to keep our balance, but the difficulties of our own progress were less than those experienced in getting the beasts forward, in raising them when they fell, which they did at every other step, in reloading them, coaxing them on, and rescuing the more valuable portions of their loads when the beasts at last fell exhausted to rise no more. Our attempts to find firmer ground nearer the mountains were all in vain. The soil there seemed more saturated than ever, and we soon gave up trying.

What we had to do was to reach the Dangla Mountains as soon as possible. Their rocky and frozen sides afforded a haven of refuge. Of the fifty mules that we had with us when we began crossing this sea of mud, only six remained when we reached a wide and long valley with a gentle slope, which led on to one of the snowy passes lying to the south-east of the great semi-circle, formed by the Dangla Mountains to the north.

For two days hail had been falling incessantly; but a few minutes after our weary feet rested once more on solid ground the sky cleared suddenly, and there was even a gleam of sunshine.

We were more like a shipwrecked crew than an exploring caravan. Nearly all our provisions had vanished, and the caravan had about four days' nourishment, consisting of flour, rice, and millet. We had not a scrap of meat, and the few peas intended for the surviving mules had perished with the animal that carried them. Many of our cases containing Mongol and Tibetan curiosities were buried deep in the mud, and at first this loss distressed us more than that of the provisions. We soon altered our opinion; but at the time we hoped to be able to shoot enough game to satisfy our needs. One by one we had been compelled to leave our poor mules to the dismal fate of burial in the mud. One by one they had formed for a time a black patch on the red mire, for an hour or more, staring straight in front, their large eyes full of terror, and one by one they had disappeared. The sight was most distressing, and we were not cheered by the thought of what our own fate must be, if all our beasts of burden were destined to perish in this manner.

On 27th August we began the ascent of the Dangla Mountains from the east, and not by the western passes. We wished to make sure of striking the Yang-tse again after crossing these great intertwining glaciers. We met with no great trouble at first, and the valley along which we went, though sloping steeply upward, seemed a real velvet carpet after the awful road of the last three days. The rocky ground showed no tracks, and it was a pleasure to step out without sinking in the mud.

For seven hours we marched between the mountain chains, the peaks of which grew ever nearer and whiter, and, after a last hard climb of some half an hour's duration, the loose stones slipping under our feet, we reached the glacier at the top of the pass. Just at first I thought we could not cross it, for we could not expect our beasts to scale a precipitous glacier; but I luckily found, on careful examination, a small patch to the side, between an old moraine and the mass of ice. We directed the caravan along this, and we reached the top of the glacier; the view was magnificent.

To the north we could detect, in the far distance, the lines of the plain and of the mud which had cost us so much. To the east and west were the innumerable snow peaks, and, lastly, to the south the glacier which we had climbed, ran down from valley to valley in waves of ice to several hundred yards below the level on which we stood. A blazing sun, such as we were not to see again for weeks, shone on the crest of the glacier, and the wild and fantastic *coup d'œil* partly repaid us for the troubles we had undergone.

Going down that dangerously steep bed of a torrent formed under the glacier by the melting snow we reached its southern base, and encamped there, near a scanty growth of grass, which could not satisfy the needs of our sorely reduced number of beasts. I calculated with my instruments the height of the pass and of our camp. The height of the top of the glacier was 20,600 feet, and that of the camp 19,300.

In spite of the altitude, and of our famine-stricken state, we were not uncomfortable, and should have enjoyed a well-earned rest had not several men at nightfall reported the absence of Lao Chang. I had last seen him toiling up the last stage of the glacier, and, as he was clearly exhausted, had unloaded a mule and sent it to bring him safe to camp. Since then no one had seen him. He could not have lost his way, for our tracks on the snow were plain enough, and his disappearance was inexplicable. It was the more surprising since, in spite of his constant fatigue, he had an excellent appetite, and no one had ever known him be a minute late for a meal. I hoped that he would turn up in the morning with his mule, having simply slept out all night; but by eight o'clock he had given no sign of life, and I sent a search party consisting of two men, with two mules, and some food to the spot where I had last seen him. I deplored the necessity of wasting a day at such a height and in such an inhospitable spot. There were no traces of game, and we had only two days' provisions. To complete the situation, the rain had begun again, and was only interrupted by hail. We waited all day for the return of the men. They came in the evening, but without Lao Chang.

It was a tedious and difficult matter to extract their story from them. They kept interjecting lugubrious expressions peculiar to the Chinese. We concluded at last that Lao Chang had committed suicide by throwing himself down a sheer precipice of some 50 feet. The mule had been found nearly dead of cold and hunger, and shivering from the rain and hail, and some traces left by the unfortunate man's fur boots had led the investigators to the brink of the precipice.

This tragic death shocked us greatly. Not only was it sad to lose a member of the caravan while still so far from our goal, but the moral effect on the survivors was incalculable. The

OUR MEN, AFTER THE DEATH OF LAO CHANG.

[*To face p.* 272.

men, already sufficiently out of hand, would become more so, and we dreaded an epidemic of suicide. The situation was certainly a wretched one for them. They had lost all hope of ever seeing their country again, and when I promised them a return voyage in a steamer from India to China they shook their heads sadly, and said to one another that they would never see India. I spent over an hour that night in their tent trying to encourage them; but I felt when I left them that I had wasted my time.

The next day, after going down a valley running from south-east to north-west, in the evening we reached the banks of the Yang-tse. But it was a very different river here. Instead of the imposing channel of water we had not been able to follow, we found a river split up sometimes into two, sometimes into three, streams, in the middle of a vast plain stretching from east to west, and easy to traverse. The Dangla Mountains obviously send down large tributaries into that portion of the river which we had missed.

Exactly east of the site of our tent a great break in the mountain circle showed where the Yang-tse cleaves its way. There was pasturage here and there on its banks, and our beasts derived some nourishment from it. In spite of the steady rain, we felt sufficiently cheerful to light a fire, and, by burning two of our boxes, we procured a fine blaze, before which we tried to dry our soaked rags. I say rags, for our Chinese sheepskin clothes had lost both shape and colour.

Some yaks were feeding about a mile away, and though very tired, I went out after them, for we had literally nothing to eat. Unfortunately, there was no chance of stalking them on the huge open plain, and they cantered off before I could get within range, thus depriving us of our hopes of a much-needed dinner.

During the next two days, we covered about 30 miles to the south - west. The view was bounded on all sides by glaciers, and after the firm ground of the plain in which we had rejoined the great river displayed fresh stretches of mud. But these we were able to escape by marching in the river bed itself, some 2 or 3 yards from the bank. The water was shallow, and in spite of the rain, the small tributaries flowing continually into it contributed very little to the volume of the stream.

Towards evening, on the second day, we reached a strange and unique country. Hills of red mud rose on all sides, some very large and lofty, others no bigger than seaside dunes in Europe. I made an attempt to scale one, and sank in up to the knees. We went on, therefore, in the river bed. And as evening closed in, and dark clouds were gathering ominously overhead, we hastily ordered our tents to be pitched on a small platform of rock which lay very handy 100 yards from the river.

The storm did not burst immediately. The night fell thick and heavy; not a breath of wind relieved the electric tension, and at midnight a loud clap of thunder resounded very near us. It was the herald of the most violent storm we have ever seen. The claps of thunder followed one another like the reports of guns in action. The lightning was so bright and vivid that it might have been midday. The sky and earth seemed about to unite at this height of 19,000 feet, and, as if in protest against our audacity in profaning these virgin altitudes, the brass spikes on our tents threw off tongues of fire several inches in length, with a terrifying crackling.

The soaked canvas acted as a conductor between the spikes and the ground, and made our position inside the tent untenable. So we had to move out under the rain and snow which fell for the greater part of this alarming night. The animals, half buried in snow, made no movement. Huddled together some paces from the tents, they watched the falling flakes covering the few tufts of grass on which they might have fed. As for ourselves, we had only half a pound of flour, which we soaked in water, and made into a kind of cake. We had not even any salt, the cook having stolen the last of it while we slept.

On the next morning, 1st September, we left the glacier, from which the Yang-tse rises on our right, two hours after breaking up camp, and crossed a water-parting on the crest of a side *arète* of the Dangla Mountains. The source of the Yang-tse is nearly in the middle of this *arète*, and the saddle-shaped pass which was surmounted by us, stretched from the glaciers that feed the great river to another group of less importance.

We had therefore accomplished one of our main objects in visiting Tibet. We now had to reach India, and the opposition of the Tibetans would perhaps intensify the natural difficulties of the task.

Above all, we had at any cost to find food. Our last handful of flour was finished.

THE YANG-TSE-KIANG IN TIBET.

[*To face p.* 276.

CHAPTER XI

THE ROAD TO INDIA

On the other side of the pass we found to our surprise a long gentle slope, crossed here and there by rivulets. The bare ground near the top changed as we went down to a luxuriant grass prairie. We reached it at six in the evening, after a march which our exhaustion had rendered slow and uncertain. We hoped to find wild yaks feeding in this abundant pasture; but we hoped in vain. There was no trace of game, and we had to march all through 2nd September without any sustenance, still moving to the south-west.

The cast of the journey, and our hopes of killing a yak, enabled us to cover over 20 miles on this day. But we met with no luck, and again lay down famished.

As this could not go on, and I had noticed what I took to be sure proof that a herd of yaks was not far away, I decided to encamp where we were for another day, and to go out in search of them.

I went down one of the many valleys where the tracks were numerous, and within 200 yards saw a herd of thirty peacefully browsing. I was well within range, and brought down a big beast, while the rest fled. I carried my news back to camp, and put fresh life into everybody. The men, who were dozing for want of better occupation, sprang up, and four of them went off at once with their knives to cut the yak up into beefsteaks. Others broke up our last boxes, and made firewood of everything not absolutely necessary to our progress.

At last we were able to rest and eat a little, for we could allow one day for it. Many of the men were in a sad condition of exhaustion and despondency. Want of food and sleep during the last few days had made things worse. But one day's rest was not much. It would have taken a week or two to rest the men thoroughly, and we could not spare the time.

We knew we must be approaching the first Tibetan settlement north of the lakes, and I was afraid that the authorities at Lhasa, who were at present unaware of our journey, would hear of it and stop it, if I did not press on south at once, as they had stopped all previous explorers in Tibet and Central Asia.

For two days we travelled south, following a river which we hoped would flow into one of the great central lakes. Its winding coast made us cover twice the distance that we should have had to traverse had we gone straight.

Traces of life appeared more and more often.

We came across freshly marked tracks, and the *débris* left by caravans.

Once we even found on the site of a camp a kind of oven, hastily constructed with square blocks of clay, in which a fire had been recently burning, for the wind had not yet entirely scattered the ashes. Our ears were soon greeted by loud barking, and several large Tibetan mastiffs rushed towards the caravan, from behind a hillock on which some tame yaks and ponies were feeding. The noise made by the dogs attracted the attention of their owners. They emerged one by one from a black tent made of yak's hide, and slowly approached us. One of them, a lama, spoke a few words to us in Chinese, and seemed satisfied with our reply. We told him we were merchants on our way to India. Unfortunately we had lost nearly all our goods in the mud, and were now reduced to great poverty. He then offered us milk and butter, and, as we had long been deprived of these luxuries, we did not scrutinise them too closely for the presence of foreign ingredients.

These people were as peaceful and amicable as possible, and it looked well for the future. The Lhasa authorities had evidently issued no orders about us, and our friends saw nothing out of the way in our arrival, though they were surprised that we had not followed the usual caravan route. We explained this as well as we could by professing to have lost our way.

But, towards evening, three men, among them

the lama in his yellow robe, saddled their ponies and rode off at a moderate pace southward. They evidently proposed to discharge their duty as sentinels by warning the soldiers of our arrival. These latter were posted near the lake Amdo-tsonak, which, according to our new neighbours, was very close.

Nothing happened that night, but I kept watch. I feared that some of our animals might be stolen under cover of the darkness. Poor and exhausted as they were, we could not have progressed without them.

Early next morning we left the little Tibetan camp and continued without any opposition to follow the winding course of the river. It was a hard day, for a drenching rain fell, and we had to cross the stream often. The water varied in depth from 3 to 4 feet, and our condition towards evening can be imagined. The rain and the stream had soaked us through, and the temperature was very little above freezing point.

We had not the slightest idea where we were, for we could see nothing through the rain; but we noticed that the valley had become a little wider.

We were awakened in the morning by the clatter of horses, apparently ridden hard, and, rushing out, we saw ten Tibetan soldiers, who had dismounted from their wild shaggy steeds, and were advancing upon the tent carrying their long rifles on their shoulders or under their arms. Of course none of our people were on the look-out, and my first act was to kick some of them awake. But for our own anxiety, we should have laughed at the expression on their faces when they saw the armed Tibetans.

We thought at first that our march would be arrested, and considering our exhausted condition, I contemplated with horror a journey to Kashmir from this place. But the soldiers on reaching the tent saluted us amicably. One of them spoke Chinese, and an animated conversation ensued, for a Tibetan in addressing a stranger thinks it necessary to use many explanatory gestures. At first we were bombarded with questions as to who we were, whence we had come, and whither we were going. I replied in a fashion that satisfied everybody, and then put some questions myself. I found that our visitors were under the orders of a petty chief, whose business it was to watch the pass through which we had come into the great lake district. As we were merchants he had no desire to stop us, and after an hour's conversation he wished us a pleasant journey. Before leaving he sold us a lb. of flour for a *tael* — an exorbitant price in Tibet. But then everybody must live somehow!

We started again with a light heart. Lhasa did not oppose us, and probably knew nothing about us. We congratulated ourselves once more on having obtained at Pekin passports for Chinese Turkestan, and on not having breathed a word about our intention of entering the forbidden precincts of Tibet. The soldiers and their chief had clearly no suspicion, and would not send a special message about us to Lhasa. By moving quickly we should probably cross the dangerous part before any orders could be issued to stop us. Our expectations were justified by the event.

The district of Amdo-tsonak, which we had now entered, was very different from the country of rocks and valleys through which we had just passed. A green plain stretched away out of sight, covered with flocks and tents, and horsemen were to be seen everywhere. From the tents rose little columns of smoke. The general impression of life and comparative wealth were a great relief after the absolutely deserted region we had traversed, meeting only one pilgrim caravan and the yak hunters.

During the day we counted sixty black tents scattered about, sometimes together, but usually at long intervals. Tibetan civilisation on the upper plateau evidently tends to the formation of little groups, consisting each of one family, rather than to larger gatherings.

The Chinese call these Tibetans "the Black Tents," because of the unvarying colour of their dwellings. They have the reputation of being extremely savage, and of pitilessly attacking travellers; we were lucky enough to have no trouble with them. On the contrary, we were always well received, and saluted when we passed a tent without entering it. Only once did we excite the anger of an old lama, by taking the caravan over the ground where his flock was folded for the night. This is a serious affront to their superstition, and we were very careful not to repeat the mistake. Occasionally riders galloped up to us from neighbouring tents, and followed us for some miles, with no show of hostility, only with the natural curiosity excited in these big children by the passing of a caravan.

During two days' march we were still in sight of Amdo-tsonak, though leaving it on our left, and towards evening on the second day we came into a mountainous region, due to a meeting of several small chains, and quite different from the long regular chains that we met with later.

A strange phenomenon was observed here by many of my men. Their feet and legs grew hard and swollen, and, so far as a Chinese skin permitted, also red. This peculiar trouble lasted about two days, without otherwise affecting the persons seized with it. At first I thought it due to the elevation, but discarded this idea when I remembered that we had been much higher without anybody suffering in this way. It was probably blood poisoning, due to the sting of some insect, but the inhabitants, when consulted, did not seem to have seen similar cases. What struck me most was that the swellings gave no pain, and did not interfere with marching.

On 8th September we reached lake Bum-tso. Its neighbourhood is fairly populous, not so much so as that of Amdo-tsonak. Here we held amicable converse with several Tibetans who showed no surprise at the sight of a sextant and an artificial horizon.

One of them, indeed, said that he had witnessed the taking of a latitude by a European who had been stopped by the Tibetan authorities a little to the south of where we were. From this man's account the traveller must have been Dr Sven Hedin. From this affable Tibetan we bought 2 lbs. of butter and two sheep for some 13 yards of Chinese linen, of which we still possessed a little. It was common blue "pou," but in Tibet the cheapest stuffs are valuable, owing to the paucity of communication.

All this part of Tibet is well populated and very fertile, at least as regards pasturage. It is not cultivated, the only occupation of the inhabitants being the raising of cattle. The temperature was cold at night, but pleasant enough by day when there was no rain, and this was due to the fact that we had come down about 2,500 feet. We were now in the temperate zone of the Tibetan plateau.

On 9th September we bade a heated farewell to the Tibetans, whose eagerness to help us in packing and in loading our mules had given them the opportunity of pilfering various small articles. We hoisted Siao Chang on to our last camel. His condition of exhaustion was growing hourly worse, in spite of all care and medicine.

Going straight south we surmounted a couple of crests, and crossed the valley in which Sven Hedin was stopped and detained more or less as a prisoner for some days. There must be a small permanent police post here, for two soldiers came up to us, bearing the Tibetan head-dress; so like the pointed cap of the mediæval alchemist. They put some questions, but let us proceed readily when they saw that we were not, like the great explorer, going towards Lhasa. This was very good luck, and we had no doubt now that we should soon be looking down upon the plains of India. But we had many miles to cover yet, and the neighbourhood of the Tengri-nor had an evil repute. The Prince of Orleans and Littledale were stopped there.

Having emerged from a labyrinth of small hills which gave us much trouble, and made us continually retrace our steps with no small irritation, we saw the blue surface of the little lake To-ko-tso gleaming in front of us. It is a pretty sheet of water, like a Swiss lake. There is a rocky island in it on which hundreds of white gulls alight.

In spite of the suggestions of the maps, I do not believe that there is any connection between the To-ko-tso and the Bum-tso, the latter lying to the south, and about 90 feet lower.

The Bum-tso is a much larger lake than the To-ko-tso, but is evidently disappearing, as is proved by the old water marks, which are very clear upon its banks. The two lakes must have been connected once, where they are now separated, by a low ridge. The water of both is salt; but a boiling spring of fresh water gushes from a rock which stands in the Bum-tso, near its north-western shore. The Bum-tso is surrounded by high mountains. There is little pasturage near it, and this, with the scarcity of fresh water, accounts for the fact that Tibetans are rarely met with near it.

We encamped, however, close to a small fort in which two Tibetans dwell by themselves. They asked us in Chinese, without leaving their post, whether we were followers of the Grand Lama of Sining, who had passed along the caravan road a few days before. When we said yes, they wished us good luck, and retired to their den.

A sad incident now cast a gloom over our successful march. Siao Chang was found dead and already stiff, at eleven o'clock at night, by one of the men who, on getting up to leave the tent, stumbled over his body. He called me, and I came and certified that the poor fellow had died from some form of heart disease.

The caravan drivers gradually collected in a sympathetic group, but no one would touch the body, and I had to wrap it in a sort of winding sheet, and use great severity of speech to induce his companions to lift the dead man and carry him a furlong away, to a specially wild and rocky spot. Here I hoped the Tibetans would not notice the recently turned ground, and that the grave would not be rifled—with a view to the theft of

THE LAKE OF TO-KO-TSO.

[*To face p.* 286.

rings or clothing, a feat they are very ready to perform if they get the chance. To dig the grave took us several hours. It was very difficult work, for the ground was frozen, and we did not wish to attract too much attention. Towards three o'clock in the morning, however, all was done, and Siao Chang was laid to rest very far from his native country, Liang-chou.

During the few months that he had been with us, Siao Chang had borne a very bad character. He lied and stole with wonderful perseverance, in spite of the punishment which invariably followed upon his offences. I had often wished to dismiss him while still near Liang-chou, but the others had pleaded so hard for him that I relented. I was further induced to keep him by his production of a letter of recommendation from a missionary. I could hardly believe that it had been given simply to get rid of him. Yet such was the case.

His was the second death, and it demoralised the rest, if possible, further, for I had to threaten them with my revolver on the next day to get them to start.

All day long the men did not interchange a word. They did their work with an eye fixed on me, in order to seize any chance of slipping behind a rock to go to sleep or die of hunger, which seemed to them a better fate than to follow me.

For two days after passing the Bum-tso, we moved south-south-west, in a direction which, if my calculations were correct, would bring us to the middle of the northern shore of the great lake. We moved at an easy pace, a little over 2 miles an hour. The sad state of our mules made several halts necessary. The country was more and more intercepted by small marshes, near which were great stretches of grass on which large flocks fed. Although we often passed only a few yards from an inhabited tent, nobody evinced the least surprise, or asked us any questions.

On 13th September, at nightfall, we saw the Tengri-nor stretching in all its magnificence before us. It was a noble sight. A great mountain chain, 100 miles long, and always ice-bound, rose behind its waste of deep blue waters. The highest peaks were reflected in the calm transparent lake, the topmost being not less than 25,000 feet high. These mighty heights form a more imposing framework than any Swiss lake can boast. Perhaps in another fifty years tourists will fly from the heat of India to refresh themselves by the Tengri-nor. The world changes so quickly nowadays that such a development would scarcely astonish one. But the altitude of 16,000 feet, which many people cannot stand, will always spoil it as a health resort.

The country on the north of the Tengri-nor is full of life. There are large collections of tents gathered round small temples, in which lamas burn incense night and day. It was strange to smell the scent after our long days in an atmosphere free from any odour of human concoction.

The plant from which they extract the incense

grows abundantly on the banks of the lake, and the sale of it is one of the only industries. It sheds a peculiar perfume, and rises to the height of a small bush.

For two days we had to let the caravan rest. Men and animals were equally exhausted, and though my wife set them a gallant example of courage and endurance, I did not desire to overtax her strength. Moreover, these days were peaceful and quiet. Some Tibetans came to see us, and sold us some sheep. They gave us all the information we wanted about the country, and no Lhasa soldier showed his peaked cap.

One of the mistakes on the maps which mark the Tengri-nor is to print a group of islands to the north-west. As we went along we could make certain that these islands do not exist. But there is a thin tongue of earth connecting a group of rocks with the land, rising so little above the surface that it is invisible at a short distance.

It was not easy to go round the lake from the middle of the northern shore to the south-western end. The ground was firm enough, and the pasturage excellent, but we had to cross several rivers which flow into the lake, their beds were often muddy, and in places there were quicksands. One in particular ran over white limestone sand, from which we had great trouble in extricating our beasts, which were now too weak to compass such difficulties without assistance.

September 17th was a day full of incident.

We had left the Tengri-nor in the morning, and began a march almost due south across a series of hills and valleys in regular lines, but so close together that one could not see more than a few furlongs either way. This favoured the laziness of the men, who tried more than once to slip out of sight. One of them, Hin, showed real ability in eluding my watchful eye.

Towards noon, having ordered a few minutes' halt, I saw Hin stretch himself out and go to sleep. When the caravan started again he took a few steps, and then began to limp. He came and asked me for a few moments in which to fix a boot which was hurting his foot. I gave him leave and waited patiently, amused at his calling the rag that swathed his foot a boot. But as time went on my patience went with it, and I ordered an advance, leaving Hin behind. He was to follow at once. We saw him no more. Shishi, our faithful watch-dog, was with him, and when towards evening she was still absent, I am afraid I regretted the loss of the dog more than that of the man. She had often warned us of danger while the men slept, and we could not do without her in this populous part.

Shortly after Hin's disappearance another man, Tchrung, stayed behind, ostensibly to look after a favourite mule which had fallen exhausted. While I went back as quickly as possible to bid Tchrung follow at once, a cousin of his, with another driver named Tatchrung, a fairly bad character, left from the front of the caravan in spite of my wife's orders, and undertook to search for the missing man. Of course they lost their way, since all the hills were just alike, so that when I came up again, tired out, I found only three men. The situation was not pleasant, seeing that the mule, by which Tchrung had stopped, carried the cartridges and what was left of our silver *taels*. Having found Tchrung, and forced him to resume his march, I had been obliged to leave him behind again, for my presence was required at the front. His promises to come quickly sounded so genuine that I had left with him the precious cartridges, and the still more precious *taels*.

If the Tibetans had attacked us that night we should have vanished from this world without being able to offer the least resistance, and the thought of it was enough to keep us awake all night.

As soon as the sun had risen I went out to look for the missing man. I hoped that having spent an icy night in the open without food, and exposed to the attacks of wolves and bears, they had learnt their lesson, and when I saw their downcast faces and outspread hands begging pardon, I felt certain that, at any rate for some days, they would have no more ideas of suicide or voluntary starvation.

But there was still no sign of Hin. We waited all day on the 18th for him, but the poor fool never arrived, and we were obliged to leave him to his fate. If we had decided to go back and find him the caravan would have mutinied.

The next day we had to cross frozen passes in a heavy fall of snow, so that the arrival of Shishi in the middle of the afternoon was the more miraculous. We suddenly heard a joyous bark, and directly afterwards, our good little dog was with us, unable to express her pleasure sufficiently. It was a wonderful feat to have followed us through the snow and over the streams, but she had already often shown exceptional sagacity. Round her neck was a bit of thin rope that she had bitten through, and this confirmed our worst fears about Hin. He had died of cold in the night; Shishi had then freed herself and come up with us. Exhaustion had now claimed three victims, and it was time to reach our goal. But we were still ten days' march from the Brahmaputra, the great artery of Southern Tibet. Judging from the general appearance of the country, and the information of the inhabitants, we could not take a straight line for the river especially in our exhausted state. A mountainous tract, very intricate and difficult, offered an inseparable obstacle, we therefore decided to follow the first stream which seemed to flow towards the Brahmaputra.

So we went for several days down a continually widening river called the Shang Chu, along whose banks little by little civilisation began to appear. The tents were larger, the people seemed more

TIBETAN PEOPLE, NEAR NAMLING.

[*To face p.* 292.

wealthy, the women's dress was more ornamental, and several wore jewels. But their greater prosperity did not make them more friendly. One day, wishing to buy a horse, we approached a tent. All its inhabitants fled to the mountains in terror. We went into it and found an old blind woman alone in a corner. We took all we wanted, and left a silver shoe on the threshold. Another day we were stopped by a little group of mounted men, a sergeant and three soldiers, who assured us that we could not go on down the river, for the way was blocked by a precipitous rock. He very kindly offered to bring us some tame yaks next day, with which to cross the river, which was now fairly deep. We took his advice, and had to admit later that he was right.

Here and there to our surprise and delight were shrubs, sometimes several feet high. Herds of tame yaks abounded, white, black, and grey, going down our way, loaded with butter and dried meat. Only very few people spoke to us, and the further we advanced the more it seemed to us that we were regarded with suspicion, if not with hostility. We were approaching the district which had felt the effects of the English expedition to Lhasa, and our presence as Europeans was noted and resented much more keenly than in the central lake country.

However, nothing important occurred till we reached the fort of Namling, rising in all its might and sanctity on the summit of a hill in the shape of a truncated cone. Under the shelter of its grey stone walls, a monastery containing three hundred Tibetan monks dominated the town proper, which had a population of one thousand. To get to it we had to use a bridge made of large iron rings stretched between two small towers, and bound together underneath with strips of yak's hide, on which wooden planks were loosely fitted. To cross this required great care and some courage in the inexperienced, for in the middle of this antique suspension bridge the chains began to swing to and fro and up and down, producing a feeling of insecurity which was increased, by the sight of the river rushing below.

As soon as we had set up our tents the lamas ordered all the people to shut their doors in our faces, and to refuse to sell us anything whatever. As we were very hungry I thought it best to supply ourselves and to ignore the veto of the lamas. Accordingly I fired on a flock of sheep, and killed three. A little later, as we were beginning to feast on mutton and buttered cake, a deputation of lamas appeared, offering us eggs and chickens; my shots had proved most effective.

Namling lies in a bend of the river, and for long distances up and down one can see old Tibetan forts, very like the castles on the Rhine. Perched on almost inaccessible cliffs, they speak well for the skill of their builders, and for the fighting spirit of former days.

Namling is one of the strongest forts north of

CROSSING THE BRAHMAPUTRA.

[To face p. 294.

THE FORT AND THE BRIDGE OF NAMLING DJONG AT THE WEST OF LHASA.

To face p. 294.

the Brahmaputra. The English expedition did not come that way.

The friendly, if compulsory, visit of the lamas resulted in the gathering of the whole population at our tents, and we were soon surrounded by hundreds. The women were naturally the boldest and most inquisitive. They wore very clean clothes and pretty jewellery. Having left the tent for a moment to give some orders I found three of them on my return investigating the contents of our bag, which had by this time been reduced to a minimum.

To crown all a troop of jugglers arrived, and went through their programme. We fell asleep with the sound of their sonorous and monotonous drums still in our ears.

From Namling to the Brahmaputra the journey was easy, for we had bought some tame yaks, and our poor remaining three mules could rest at last.

We crossed the river in square boats, made of yak hide stretched over a framework of wood. It was the most dangerous craft conceivable, and I do not understand yet how we induced our last and only camel to enter and stay in it. We proposed to offer this animal to the Calcutta Zoological Gardens as a product of the north.

The yaks also were difficult to manage. The boatmen had tied them all to the stern of one of the boats, and as soon as they started swimming each chose a different direction, so that the embarkation amid these distractions very nearly came to grief.

In the evening we encamped near Shigatse, and, four days later, we saluted the English flag flying at Gyantse.

I will not say much about this portion of Tibet. The fertile fields, stone houses, manners and customs of it have been well described in excellent books. Since the Tibetan expedition the country south of the Brahmaputra is well known, except along that portion of its course which is intercepted by rapids, and another portion to the north-west of the point where it crosses the Indian frontier.

The general aspect of the country is quite different from that of the northern part. Relative cultivation and wealth have worked great changes. Tibet, the true Tibet, the Tibet of the adventurous explorer, lies to the north, as completely ice-bound and desolate as Southern Tibet is smiling and attractive.

At Gyantse Captain O'Connor, the political agent who remained there after the expedition, entertained us most kindly for several days, and, when we had received permission from the Government of India to proceed south, we came into Sikkim, and became the guests of Mr Claude White, the political agent there. Here we enjoyed the greatest hospitality amid the lovely scenery and flowers of Sikkim, and we spent some days at Gantok in infinite peace, with the pleasant

THE TEMPLE AND FORT OF GYANTSE.

[To face p. 296.

feeling of having succeeded at all points in our long and dangerous journey; of having for the first time crossed Tibet from north to south, and of having entered India from China, while all others who had attempted this had met with pitiable failure.

THE END

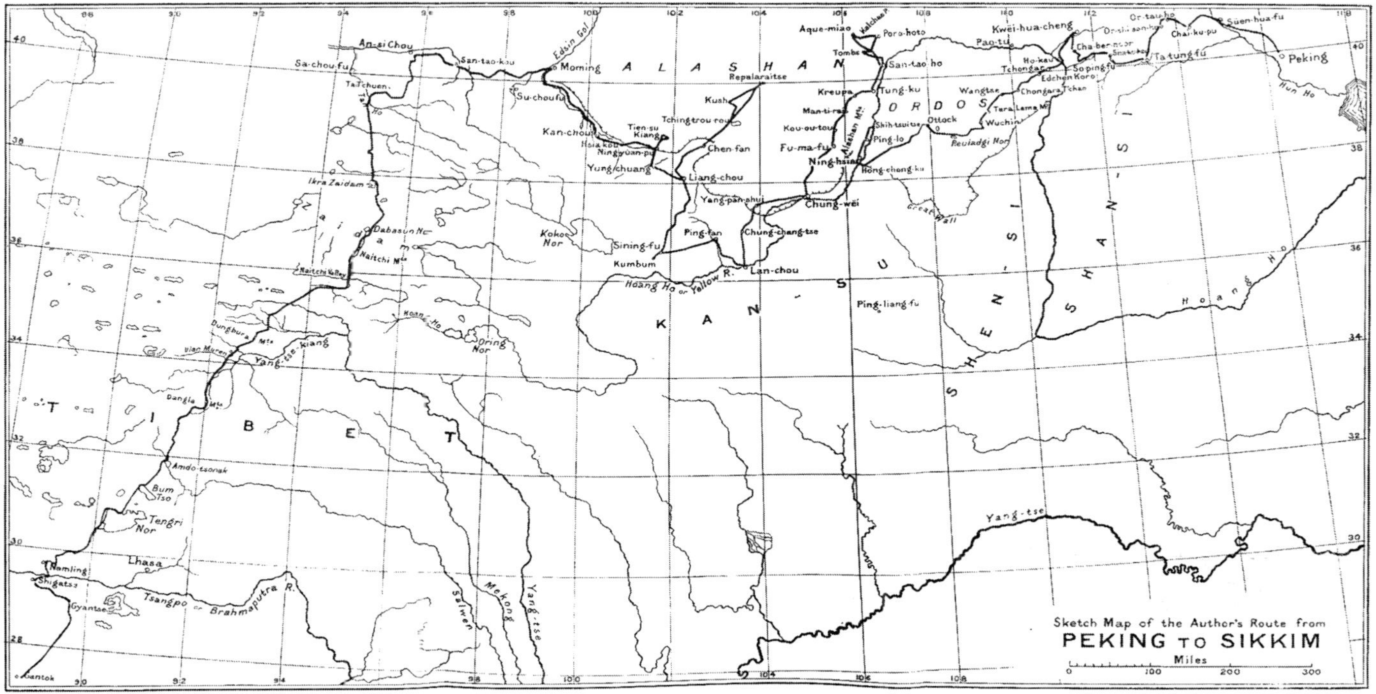

Sketch Map of the Author's Route from
PEKING TO SIKKIM
Miles
0
100
200
300
Peking
Süen-hua-fu
Chai-ku-pu
Ta-tung-fu
So-ping-fu
Kwei-hua-cheng
Pao-tu
Ho-kau
Tchongar
Edchen Koro
Chongara Tchan
Wangtse
Tara Lama Mi
Wuchin
Reuiadgi Nor
Ottock
ORDOS
Aque-miao
Poro-hoto
Tombe
San-tao-ho
Tung-ku
Kreupa
Man-ti-ras
Kou-ou-tou
Shih-tsui-tse
Ping-lo
Fu-ma-fu
Alashan Mts
Ning-hsia
Hong-cheng-ku
Chung-wei
Great Wall
ALASHAN
Repalaraitse
Kush
Tching-trou-rou
Chen-fan
Liang-chou
Yang-pan-shui
Chung-chang-tse
Ping-fan
Sining-fu
Kumbum
Lan-chou
Hoang Ho or Yellow R.
Ping-liang-fu
KAN SU
SHEN SI
SHAN SI
Hoang Ho
Tien-su
Kiang
Hsia-kou
Ning-yuan-pu
Yung-chuang
Kan-chou
Su-chou-fu
Moming
Edsin Gol
San-tao-kou
An-si Chou
Sa-chou-fu
Ta-Tchuen
Tai Ho
Ikra Zaidam
Zaidam
Dabasun Nor
Naitchi Mts
Naitchi Valley
Koko Nor
Hoang Ho
Oring Nor
Dungbura Mts
Ulan Muren
Yang-tse-kiang
Dangla Mts
TIBET
Amdo-tsonak
Bum Tso
Tengri Nor
Lhasa
Namling
Shigatse
Gyantse
Tsangpo or Brahmaputra R.
Salwen
Mekong
Yang-tse
Gantok

INDEX